Joywords

Joywords

An Invitation to Happiness through an Introduction to the Option Method

Frank Mosca

Writers Club Press
San Jose New York Lincoln Shanghai

Joywords
An Invitation to Happiness through
an Introduction to the Option Method

Writers Club Press
an imprint of iUniverse.com, Inc.

For information address:
iUniverse.com, Inc.
5220 S 16th, Ste. 200
Lincoln, NE 68512
www.iuniverse.com

ISBN: 0-595-15780-7

Printed in the United States of America

Contents

Introduction

A "Chance" Meeting That Changed My Life!

It was a hall full of therapists, healers of every stamp and people were taking turns describing themselves. Up stood a man who identified himself as an "Option" educator. My ears perked up, because I was acquainted with the title from another encounter years before, and I made it a point to speak to him when the general meeting was ended. That in itself began an important friendship, but that is not the point of this tale. He began to tell me of a man, Bruce Di Marsico, who created the approach to life called the Option Method. And so, I contacted Bruce and made arrangements to see him; something truly wonderful, intense and transformational ensued from the first few moments of our meetings. I had already gained my life back from the edge of despair through work I had done in the years prior to these meetings, but now, in literally minutes, doubts, suspicions, beliefs that had lingered like aches and sometimes rose up in eruptions of pain and terror, disappeared, vanished. Somehow any last vestige of a belief that I was not fully, totally and forever entitled to feel completely happy now in this moment and all moments that I would want it without reservation...ALL THAT SIMPLY WAS GONE. And, like a spark touching the driest tinder, I exploded in a conflagration of good feelings!

I continued my work with him, now as an intense student of his brilliant vision of happiness and it is that vision, to the degree that I can make it manifest from my own attitude of happiness and my own experience of helping people, that this book is dedicated to bringing to you, dear reader. My words will speak the truth of happiness as I have come to know it, and

Bruce's words, to the extent they reside in the quotes that will accompany my text, will speak for him. Bruce's voice fell silent with his death in 1995 and I do not claim in any way to be his voice, nor do I claim that my manner of dealing with people in the dialogues to follow are reflective of how he would deal with people in the same situation; but, I am most happy to share what I can if you have a desire to travel along with me. Obviously, the names and circumstances of the people in the Dialogues have been altered to preserve their privacy. Also, keep in mind that this is an introduction and in no way pretends to be exhaustive. Indeed, as you might eventually come to know, there is a vast world of subtle good feelings and knowingness about both the nature of unhappiness and happiness which this book will not touch. Some of these things, more philosophically addressed in the format of literary vignettes about Good, Evil, The Meaning of History, Freedom and much more, are found in another book I have written entitled *The Unbearable Wrongness of Being: Getting Beyond the Myth of Unhappiness*. Additionally, my novel, *The Godspeak,* but even more directly, my *Joybuilding System Workbook* can be of great help in your explorations. But let me also emphasize that the basic truth about happiness is in this volume and with it, should that be what happens for you, you can make the quantum leap from unhappiness to happiness. That is the most important potential of all; what explorations await you once you have claimed your happiness is the infinite bliss of your own personal play in the fields of joy and equanimity.

Chapter One

The Beginnings

*"THE TRUTH: Therefore, the beginning point, the Great Truth we start
with, is that we know that people believe that unhappiness is necessary, and
that is why they are unhappy. It is almost beside the point to believe that people get unhappy, or make themselves unhappy......they believe they must be
unhappy, and are suffering because they believe it is an inescapable truth.
Unhappiness is simply believing; not being, or getting, or making or doing
unhappiness."*[1]

Option as a method of self transformation was brought into being by
Bruce Di Marsico sometime before 1970. It is NOT a therapy, no matter
how many people may use it that way, or might call it that. Rather, it is
more a method of self education about the truth of happiness and unhappiness. There are no diagnostic categories, no pathologies, repressed trau-
mas to uncover, no inner children to rescue, no behaviors to modify or fix,
no symptoms to relieve. Not that the attempt to deal with all these things
is not the fruit of enormous human labor and ingenuity as people try to
parse out the seemingly impenetrable mysteries of human misery. But, no,
Option has only one premise, one goal, one purpose for being: to let you
know that unhappiness is not a necessary, inevitable part of the human
landscape. The premise is quite simple but, in the face of how the over-
whelming majority of humankind experiences itself, startlingly radical:
unhappiness is not innate or immanent in the human condition. We are
unhappy because we believe we have to be!

For anyone starting out to understand this truth, immediate objections
will arise, and they will arise all based on what you feel. You will perhaps
immediately protest, at least in your mind, if not your gut, that that's not

how I experience unhappiness. I don't choose it. It just happens! And, that is precisely the problem, you might add. It just seems to happen against my will. It is called forth by the never ending multiplicity of experiences all around me, my family, friends, community, nation, world; by natural events, storms, floods; human events, plane crashes, building collapses, by diseases, murders, rejections, failures, "sins," "evil": in short by everything! These "things" of the world seem to have the power to penetrate my very self and manipulate my feelings against my will. No, unhappiness is not a choice, you might object; it is the inevitable outcome of being human. Emotions may seem for you to have some autonomous life; they may seem to rise up mysteriously from within, called forth by those around us at will, or by subtle reminders of past experience that unleash the demons of pain or of symptoms with maddening regularity.

"If you believe that something makes you unhappy, you will believe it is making you unhappy. That is what you will seem to feel. As long as you believe something will make you unhappy, you will keep experiencing the fear that it will make you unhappy."[2]

With the advent of Option, that way of understanding our selves can change. We could know that what we feel is what we believe, even when we are not in touch with that belief. Indeed, it is the genius of the Option system to gently but thoroughly expose to view the beliefs that run our experience. The fact that our responses seem so "instantaneous" is simply an artifact of the speed of our neurobiological potentials. Every emotional feeling is the result of a complex dynamic of belief processes at work, processes that are prior to the appearance of the emotion, no matter how instantaneous it may feel, i.e. "the individual is the sole determiner of his or her emotional states."[3]

The question then is how to expose these beliefs so that the connection can be made clear and so that you can actually feel differently and thereby know without having to be "convinced" somehow, that you actually are believing differently. Look, isn't it true that we all want to feel good, happy, call it what you will? Remember, by happy I simply mean any emotional feeling that you DO want and unhappy is just an umbrella term to describe any feeling that you DO NOT want to have, no matter what name you give it, fear, sadness, grief, annoyance, irritation, anger, rage, terror, jealousy, etc. The problem is that we just don't feel that we can feel happy because events somehow "conspire" to make us unhappy. But even when we feel in control of our emotions, we sometimes seem constrained to feel ways we would prefer not to feel because it is demanded of us that we feel a particular way. And, of course, for other issues, we actually want to feel the pain of outrage, grief, sadness etc., perhaps because it is seen as the badge of our humanity, compassion and empathy to respond that way so that others will know that in fact, we do care! But for the moment, let us deal with those responses that seem to require us to feel a particular way. For example, when someone tells us of some world or local event that is termed "bad" or "tragic" do we not sometimes respond with a tone of sadness or commiseration, even when we do not feel that way inside! Why do we do that? I would put forth that we do that because we want to appear a certain way in the eyes of our fellows, and to respond without the "appropriate" affect of unhappiness might leave us open to criticism as being unfeeling or uncaring. So, in some instances at least, we can identify creating the appearance of certain feelings strictly for social purposes, even when we do not particularly feel them inside.

We can also recall starting out pretending to have certain feelings, i.e., perhaps when trying to get our young children to go to bed. We put on a serious tone initially and then as our youngsters continue to dawdle and delay, we may actually "become" angry at their behavior and feel the anger instead of just acting angry. A shift has occurred and now we say that our children "made" us angry, so again we speak in the language of having feelings created in us by the actions of others. It is interesting, is it not, that when one person gets angry with another, the person toward which the anger is directed will often say: "You know, you have no reason, or alternately, there is no reason for being angry with me!" This is a telling remark, even though it is uniformly unsuccessful and usually only results in even greater anger on the part of the already angry person. This remark along with others in our linguistic tradition such as "sticks and stones may break my bones but words will never hurt me!" relates a profound truth, but one that is almost uniformly ignored. I know that when I was a child this statement was my last defense and it was inevitably followed by my tears as I indeed did feel that words could hurt me. "Believing Unhappiness is Good is Unhappy: Unhappiness is experienced because we believe that unhappiness is good, healthy, sincere, sane, moral, loving, appropriate and self-affirming when properly experienced."[4]

CULTURE IS NOT THE "ENEMY"

However, hopefully it will not in any way be understood from what I am saying that I consider Culture to be the "enemy." There is no "enemy" in some fundamental sense that there are ideas or people who have the power to somehow cause us unhappiness. There are just people, some of whom might possibly feel quite inimical to the point of view being here presented, who are following what they believe. Indeed, I understand that cultures represent the wisdom of generations congealed into the short-hand of moral imperatives and laws. I know that the generations that put those imperatives together did so believing that they represented the distillation of the best answers they could come up with to what they considered to be the nature of the human condition.

Obviously, they did not act purposely to befuddle and create misery in their people. Not at all. Compassion from an Option perspective is precisely knowing that whatever solutions an individual or a culture comes up with, however they might be poles apart from what we understand to be helpful, they still represent the best that an individual or group can do at that moment. This in no way, however, locks anyone into surrendering their options to be some other way in the next moment, I hasten to add!

If, for example, a parent should teach a child that the world is a painful, wretched place and that happiness is actually dangerous precisely because it is an "illusion" and as such is bound to explode in your face and leave you even more wounded with the knowledge of the true nature of the world, then wouldn't it be a mercy, from their perspective, to quash any incipient sign of joy or gladness, believing as they do that the child will only suffer more profoundly from the loss of the illusion, i.e. happiness. Better to exist with things as they really are and steel oneself against the icy winds of misery that blow endlessly across the existential deserts of life! WOW! Bleak, right! Yes, but the point is an important one. *"An important point to remember about the Option Method practitioner is that he/she does not believe that people SHOULD not be unhappy, or that they SHOULD be happy. The Option Method demonstrates that people chose their emotions, not that they SHOULD choose differently, but that they nevertheless truly choose, and are not victims to emotions they have no choice about."5 (capitals mine, F.M.)*

I am not out to bash any culture, group, therapy or individual. Quite the opposite, I know that it could never be "wrong" or "bad" to be unhappy no matter what the consequences. Nor do I believe in any way, shape or form that people "should" or "must" be happy! Indeed, any hint of "oughtness" or "shouldness" about the whole issue of happiness is a trap that could only become another form or version, however conceived, that "there must be something wrong with me" that I am still unhappy after having read this book about happiness! Know from me, if you should reach that conclusion, I had no intent for you to come to it and would hope you might someday come to know otherwise. For, along with the first, fresh breath of the God of Genesis I say joyously that ALL IS GOOD! If "good" has any meaning at all, it means all are doing the best they know to do given what they believe. To repeat, this is the essence of true compassion from my point of view, so let no one understand from what is said, or draw any conclusion but that I have the profoundest respect for the attempts by all cultures, communities, shamans, therapists, families, individuals to find satisfying ways to live their lives by their own lights. Having said all that, then, LET THE GAMES BEGIN! Yes, games, play, joy, frolicking and rollicking in the process of surrendering our unhappiness is what I have planned for you. No kidding. You are free to play. At most, this book is the price of admission.

EXERCISE ONE:
IDENTIFYING SOCIAL REQUIREMENTS FOR UNHAPPINESS

Just take time out or better yet take a piece of paper and recall how many times in the last days or weeks you have "acted" a certain way in order to be perceived as a person that "fits" the culturally acceptable norm. Don't worry about knowing that you are acting; that is understood. The point of the exercise is simply to recognize how many of our responses are the product of social conformity, i.e., what is demanded. You will probably still be believing that that has little to do with the feelings that just "rise up "within you and over which you believe you have no control, and the feelings of pain that you want to have to sense yourself as being human about things. That's okay. Just record all the instances where you know you were pretending to placate some social imperative.

Chapter Two

It's Only a Question of Questions When It Comes to Understanding Your Unhappiness.

The founder of the Option Method, Bruce Di Marsico, realized that his own decision to be happy was not going to be convincingly explained by the mere telling of the truth, i.e., that you don't have to be unhappy. He knew that people had to come to this themselves, through the process of unfolding the illusions of their beliefs in a way that they could plainly see and easily replicate for themselves. Hence the creation of the Option Questions, a simple Socratic method of self questioning that can pare through all the layers of objection and defensiveness and go straight to the heart of the empty cored "onion" of unhappy belief constructions. Hence, the Option Questions:

WHAT AM I UNHAPPY ABOUT?

This is the first Option question. The answer given to it may be one of an endless list of reasons, or in some instances, you may simply not know. Most times, people will give their reasons: I am unhappy because I don't have enough money, because my lover doesn't love me, because my mother was cruel to me, because I don't feel the way I want to feel about something, because, because, because….. There is no end to such reasons. We can be unhappy about anything. But, by at least asking the question, we place our initial awareness upon ourselves as a part of the equation of our unhappiness, that is I am unhappy, and that there is a reason for my unhappiness. At this point, we may uniformly place the reason outside ourselves, or we may view ourselves as being a way we "ought" not to be and therefore we become the occasion for our own unhappiness. This often only compounds our misery, because we may feel trapped by how we are into a continual cycle of life defeating ways of being. In any case, asking this first question positions our awareness such that we can then take the second question to heart.

WHAT ABOUT THAT (MEANING WHATEVER IT IS THAT I GIVE AS A REASON TO BE UNHAPPY) MAKES ME UNHAPPY?

Now we are invited to focus more intently on the reasons we have given for our unhappiness. At this point, the journey of each of us will take its own road, one which from this initial perspective is quite unpredictable and can be most revealing and ultimately liberating. Let us take one example. Three people say they are unhappy because they do not have as much money as they would want (they may say "need," but, as we shall see, that is just the way that unhappiness falsely amplifies want). One person, in answer to this first question might reply: "Not having enough money means that I will not be attractive to other people and that will mean that I will be all alone." The other person might respond to the very same reason that "not having enough money means that I am a failure and people will not have any respect for me." The third might respond " not having enough money might mean that I wouldn't be able to pay for my son's serious operation."

So now we have three people who started out with the same apparent unhappiness, namely, not having enough money. Yet when they are asked the second question, What about that makes you unhappy? they all respond with different reasons, ones that, on the surface at least, seem to branch off into different directions. So, for example, the people who are afraid that not having enough money would mean they would be alone now have specified their unhappiness to be not really a fear of not having enough money, but that it would mean they would thereby be alone. Now then, the next question would be: "What about being alone is something you would be unhappy about?"

For the person, for whom not having money meant that they were a failure and would not be respected, then the next question might be "What do you mean?" that is to try to get the person to elucidate what they mean by failure. For the third person who fears not having the money because it would deprive his son of an operation then the question would be "What about that would be unhappy for you?"

Thus each of the three people is now branching out into more and more specific instances of what they are unhappy about, so that as this is pursued, they are reducing their reasons to some more fundamental belief that they hold until they may perhaps come to the moment when they say that they don't know why they are unhappy. This is always an opportunity, because it represents a real truth: there is no reason except the reasons that we give, no matter how they are organized or layered in the logic of our belief systems. Ultimately, the only reason to be unhappy is because we believe we have to be. But let us simply test the process to see how it operates for us.

EXERCISE TWO:
HOW TO LISTEN LOVINGLY AND FOLLOW THE TRAIL OF OUR BELIEFS

Part of this exercise can be done alone, but the listening requires another person. If alone, take a piece of paper and start with the first question, What am I unhappy about? Whatever your response, write it down and then ask, "What about this makes me unhappy?" Just keep following the trail until you either run out of reasons or just seem to find a reason that will not brook any further question.

If you do this with a partner, then do yourself a favor and practice the following portion of the listening exercise to increase your skills to be present patiently and without intrusive assumptions as someone else unfolds their information to you. Remember, all you are doing is exposing as many reasons/beliefs as you can manage to find. That is the sole point of the exercise.*

LISTENING COMFORTABLY: Let one person start by making a Statement (it doesn't have to be about any "issue" but it can be). The statement should be brief, no more than two or three sentences. The other person then will repeat what the first has said in as exact a way as possible, using the first person's words as much as possible. When done, the first person will affirm whether the second's feedback of what was said was exact and contained all the salient points or not. If not, the first person will repeat it again and the process will continue until that person is completely satisfied that the second person has repeated his or her statement authentically and fully. Then the two switch roles and the speaker becomes the listener. Do this as many times as you comfortably can until you really get into the habit both of listening to what the other person says and of freely and accurately feeding it back. It helps to break the habit of anticipating what others say; the object is to let go of planning your response, rather than really being with that person. This will allow you to be an open and willing receptacle for whatever information another may be wanting to share with you. This will help greatly in conditioning you to listen to another so that you can create a helpful rhythm in asking the Option questions.

WHAT ARE YOU AFRAID WOULD HAPPEN(OR WOULD IT MEAN ANYTHING ABOUT YOU) IF YOU WERE NOT UNHAPPY ABOUT THAT (THAT IS WHATEVER YOU HAVE IDENTIFIED AS BEING WHAT YOU ARE UNHAPPY ABOUT)?

This is a question that almost always brings a look of confusion to the faces of those first questioned in this way. It is a totally unexpected question, not only in its form but because it really questions the heart of all assumptions about unhappiness. So allow yourself to really hear it and let it sink in. Let us see how it would operate in the context of the dialogue.

What about those hypothetically "unhappy about money" people. They may have traveled far from the initial stated unhappiness about money, as you undoubtedly have if you experimented in following the trail of your beliefs. However, we are going to apply the questions now in a way that would not normally apply, as you will see, in the course of a dialogue. The application here is for explanatory purposes only, i.e., to show, however premature and artificial it might seem in this context, how the question is designed to draw forth a person's understanding of their beliefs about their unhappiness.

Let's take the person who is afraid that not having money would mean that he would be alone, and let us ask the question "What are you afraid would happen if you were not unhappy about being alone?" That question has in so many instances elicited the following kind of response: " If I were not unhappy about it, then I might just settle into my being alone and not do anything about it," or "I might not care about being alone if I were not unhappy about it." Then a clarifying question could be asked: "are you saying that your way of making sure that you will not remain alone, or do nothing about being alone, is to make yourself fearful so that you will be sure to do something about it?" Now, what that individual could know is that the heart of their beliefs rests with their own construction of unhappiness, in this case fear, as a means of preventing more unhappiness.(I hasten to add that at this point the whole concept of "alone" as something bad is not yet being questioned).

The same question for the person who fears that not having enough money would mean s/he was a failure. I would clarify that word "failure," but even if I were to ask immediately "What are you afraid would happen if you were not afraid of failure," it is possible that person might answer " if I wasn't afraid of failure, then I might not do anything to avoid failing." Again the clarifying question might be: "are you saying that your way of making sure you do not experience the thing you call failure is to create the pain of fear so as not to be what you call a failure?" There once more is the possibility of knowing that we create our feelings out of our beliefs, i.e., that the thing called "failure" (which we could come to see at some point is a word without any real meaning content) is something to be avoided and the pain of fear is used to motivate that person not to ever experience that dreaded state of failure again.

The other person whose son might not have the operation for lack of money, might have another type of experience. They might answer the question "Would it mean anything about you if you were not unhappy about the prospect of not having enough money for your son's operation" by saying "God, if I were not upset about that, what kind of an unfeeling, uncaring father would I be?" The clarifying question might be "are you saying that your way of making sure that you know that you are precisely the caring, loving person that you want to be toward your son, is to be unhappy at the prospect of not being able to supply him with this operation?"

Now, we are only illustrating the way in which this question, and its many variants could be used to expose the way beliefs are used and how they are born, really, out of the cultural/social/familial requirements that have been each person's accepted legacy. Obviously, these questions are not asked in order to judge, but only to clarify how we put our unhappiness to use as a means of maintaining our inherited sense of "goodness" or "caring" or "loving" or concern of any kind. We believe we "need" these unhappy feelings to motivate, control and make morally acceptable ourselves and others.

As said earlier, in an actual Option dialogue, this last question might not arise for a while, or sometimes not at all, so that what we are after here in this initial exposure to the Option method is simply a sense of the reasons why the questions are used. Let us see for ourselves.

EXERCISE THREE:
BRINGING FORTH THE REASONS FOR OUR BELIEFS

In the last exercises we identified initially why we were unhappy; then we explored the trail of our beliefs to demonstrate how the initial sense of our unhappiness changes complexion as we question ourselves more closely. Now we can have fun seeing how many of our beliefs (using the list we have made from the previous exercise) might be amenable to the last option question. Just relax, and if you are doing this on your own, ask the question and write down your answers to what you are afraid would happen or it would mean about you were you not to be unhappy about each belief that you ended up with when following your individual trail of beliefs. See how many yield you the experience of knowing that your unhappiness, by whatever name, is what you use to ratify your goodness or worthiness or sincerity or lovingness or concern. And if you were not to be unhappy, do you believe that that would mean something about you? Do you really want to be unhappy even in the cases where the world around you seems to demand it?

If you are doing this with a friend, then see how many beliefs you can jointly identify and possibly discard, how many feelings, some that may have even seemed intractable, you can change. Really let yourself feel the wonderful freedom in your gut when some unhappiness has been surrendered. Option is not about talking around your feelings or causes from the past etc. Option is about the ACTUAL FELT EXPERIENCE OF A CHANGE! Many therapies are like bad jokes, the therapist has to continue to explain the punch line because you just didn't "get it". Option works only when it works for YOU. Only when YOU feel a difference in YOUR gut through the surrendering of some belief requiring unhappiness do you "get it" and then no one has to convince you. YOU KNOW IT!

NOTHING EVER CHANGES:
THE ILLUSION OF THE PERMANENCE OF

BELIEFS

We all have had the experience of our beliefs changing. When we are in the grips of a present belief, we often forget how many things we believed at one time and now don't even have the smallest feeling connection with. I once saw a person who had been phobic in her early teens. After getting over her phobia, she returned years later and this time was in distress because she now had begun a relationship in which she was afraid that the other person did not reciprocate her feelings. She felt desperate over this. I brought her to a street corner where years ago we had dealt with her phobia, a phobia so severe that she felt literally as if she was going to die should she enter upon and attempt to cross the street. I asked her: " Now I want you to feel as if you are going to die now when you try to cross the street." She looked at me in puzzled fashion and said: "That's impossible. I don't have any such fear any longer. I could not feel that way now." I agreed and then went on to question her beliefs about the desperate feelings she was currently feeling about her love relationship. With a little help, she was able to surrender her beliefs about that too!

EXERCISE FOUR:
IDENTIFYING BELIEFS THAT NO LONGER APPLY IN
OUR LIFE

Again, get a piece of paper and take some time to remember things that you felt passionately about years before, but have no feeling of relevance to you now. Don't choose things that you still have feelings about, but rummage through your information about yourself to identify precisely those things that do not have any emotional power. For instance, you may have believed in Santa Klaus, or had girlfriends or boyfriends or ex lovers or political or religious views which now have no emotional meaning for you. Write them down and recall how intense you were about them at the time. You can recall being intense without feeling any intensity about the recall. Linger on the list and experience the wonder of beliefs that are essentially no longer beliefs and therefore have no feeling impact. Now you know that change is possible.

Chapter Three

It All Begins with Fear

"The only thing feared is unhappiness. That is all you can fear. Fear means anticipating unhappiness. Fear, as we are using the word, is an emotion: not the desire to avoid, or the decision to avoid alone, but that, along with the belief, that if you do not you will become unhappy."[6]

Unhappiness begins with fear, the fear that one cannot be happy, the fear that forces beyond our control can take away our good feelings against our will; or, we fear that to feel happy would violate some norm or standard that would make us unacceptable in our interpersonal world. Thus we "catch 22" ourselves with conflicting imperatives that only deepen our sense of dis-ease.

FEAR AND THE "ONEROUS" O'S: OWE, OUGHT, OBLIGED! DIALOGUE ONE: SALLY: DAMNED IF I DO AND DAMNED IF I DON'T

A woman in her late thirties came to me with a complaint of initial panic attacks. She was rapidly becoming unable to travel out of a very circumscribed area and this experience was threatening every aspect of her everyday life.

Upon opening up a dialogue with her about her situation several things came to light. She was in a long term relationship with a man with whom she had had a child, but with whom she was no longer in love. Instead, she was involved with another person whom she found much more compatible and loving. She was filled with guilt about her feelings and this was exacerbated by family members warning her of dire consequences should she surrender the financial security of her first relationship. The crucial pieces of the dialogue centered around how "bad" she felt for this man, who had not shown any real interest or affection for her in years and who often was away from home for long stretches of time. The dialogue went this way: (F: being me and S: Sally)

F: What about the thought of Joe (the father of her child) being upset with you distresses you?

S: Well, he's done a lot for me over the years, despite his coldness; and after all Jenny is his child. How could I just tell him that I want out of the relationship? My Aunt Freda keeps phoning me to say how terrible that would be and how dangerous it would be to lose the financial security he represents.

F: Even if others are afraid for you, why would you personally be distressed to change the situation if you wanted to?

S: Well, I just wouldn't be fair to him to do this.

F: What do you mean "fair"?

S: You know, after all this time and his investment in the house and support and everything, to just dump him.

F: Are you saying that it would mean something about you were you to decide to leave?

S: Well, yes, I would be ungrateful.

F: What do you mean?

S: That I owe him for his time and effort with me and Jenny.

F: What do you mean by "owe"?

S: That when people do something for you that puts you in their debt. And I feel the guilt of not honoring that debt.

F: In what way did his freely doing what he wanted to do for you and your and his child put you in any position of debt to him?

S: Well, how are you supposed to respond to such actions?

F: How do you want to?

S: I'm so damned sick and tired of feeling all this obligation to everyone.

F: In what way do you feel obliged?

S: What he did binds me to him.

F: How does it do that?

S: I don't know but it just feels like it does.

F: And what are you afraid would happen if you didn't feel obligated to him as you do?

S: Well if I didn't feel obligated I would feel okay.

F: Yes, but listen to the question again: " What are you afraid would happen if you did not feel obligated?"

S: Ah, yes, well I would feel like a real ungrateful bitch if I didn't feel any sense of obligation to him.

F: So are you saying that your way of making sure you don't feel like an ungrateful bitch is by holding on to your sense of obligation?

S: Yeah, yeah. I never thought of it that way, but yeah. And that's strange isn't it?

F: What do you mean?

S: I mean that I feel really shitty and angry being obliged to him and yet, as I just saw, I do it so that I won't feel shitty and angry as an ungrateful bitch. My feeling obliged doesn't really help me to feel any better anyhow.

F: So what would it be like for you not to feel obliged?

S: Well as I sit here now I'm beginning to feel okay about that.

F: Can you really feel okay in your gut with that sense of feeling no obligation whatsoever to this man for what he has done?

S: (Pause as she thinks it over). Yes, yeah, you know I really can. But, how can that be that its okay to feel that way?

F: Do you still feel in any way that it means something about you that you don't feel obliged?

S: No, but I still feel grateful to him.

F: Is feeling grateful the same as feeling obliged?

S: (Pause as she works that out). No, no. Feeling grateful doesn't have any pain attached to it. It just seems to be acknowledging that someone was willing to do whatever they did. Joe did what he wanted to do for us, as you said earlier, freely. No one coerced him. And as far as I know, he may be supportive even when he discovers that I love someone else.

F: Wouldn't you want to know if someone didn't love you, since love is what we give freely, spontaneously.

S: Yes, that's right. I am doing him no favor just remaining an irritated, unhappy person in his life. I wouldn't want anyone, except that they freely chose to want me. I guess this is really being compassionate?

F: What do you think?

S: Yes, that's a definite yes, just allowing him to be whatever he is—that feels like compassion to me.

F: How do you feel?

S: (pause with her eyes glazed over with a gloss of tears). You know, I feel good, really good and I can' believe it, or rather I do believe it. It's just a good feeling inside.

Sally went on not only to change her relationships in an amicable and financially reasonable way, but also to discover that her panic attacks disappeared as she let go of her beliefs about how she "ought" to be in the eyes of others. It became clear to her that the panic was just the manifestation in public places of her fears of being "wrong" for herself. When she no longer felt that "wrong for me" feeling, and also felt free to attend to her own sense of how she wished to be cautious, then there was no panic to be found anywhere: "A person comfortable with their own sense of caution; who does not feel challenged to 'overcome' their so-called fear, will not feel the fear...."[7] This is an important point. All too often we are taught that we must surrender our caution to some familial or cultural imperative. Fearing shame, we choose to go against that sense of caution, all the while resenting our surrender. Thus for both men and women, we are told to measure up to the standards set by others before we have become comfortable that that represents something good for us. But the taunts of being a "wimp" or a "coward" or not sufficiently "macho" can be something we allow to intimidate us. By committing ourselves prematurely to standards of conduct that violate our sense of caution, we can develop fears, phobias, even obsessions. For while at the one and the same time we are making a show of compliance, we are also holding back out of our sense of caution which we are too fearful to acknowledge. Eventually, this initially conscious duplicity becomes hidden in our belief patterns and all we are left with is the apparently inexplicable, puzzling sense of dread and dis-ease in the many ways this might manifest itself in our lives. Now, Sally's release from this very conflict was accomplished in three sessions of one hour each. Not that this is by far always the case, but it does demonstrate that our ability to let go of what seem insurmountable issues can surprise us.

"NO ONE OWES ANYONE ANYTHING"

"If I can have no more than what I can get (and keep) by myself, then no one is to blame. There is nothing that anyone should do for me. If I trust another, then that is my choice. They do not owe me to perform or deliver for me, or be as good for me as I believe I would be for me. Neither do they owe me to be as good for me as I think they should. Each person can only act as he believes is best for himself."[8]

Another important dimension of unhappiness that got exposed in this dialogue is the illusion of being in "debt" to another. What can that mean emotionally other than that if you do not do for others what they or you say they want you to do, that then you MUST be unhappy about it. To owe is to ought is to be obliged is to feel bound, hence in a bind and of course unhappy! Sally felt that way because she believed that if she did not, that would mark her out as a "bad" person, and "ungrateful bitch" in her description.

All the "ought" words and concepts are "binding" words, concepts that are designed to foster discomfort in others, and in ourselves, as a means of trying to control our behavior, of assuring that people will follow through on their promises. Now, of course, we have, in the various human communities, laws of contract that are specifically set forth to try to ensure that human interactions will be marked by a willingness to follow through on the part of those who enter into such arrangements. So whether it is a bank, or a government or whatever entity or individual, these arrangements are ultimately backed up by the community in the form of consequences, fines or imprisonment if they are not honored. In our collective wisdom we seek to promote a pragmatically workable way of dealing with one another with some sense of certitude.

However those laws are only as valid as the community's will and capability to enforce them. That practical endeavor has nothing to do with the issue of happiness, where people are supposed to feel bad if they do not do what we want them to do. In the arena of human loving and emotional interrelating, such precepts are only painful baggage that nobody really wants, since it is but the palest substitute for what we do want, i.e. gratitude! Now, notice how Sally came to understand the difference between obligation and gratitude. The etymology of the words give away the meaning in an instant. The Latin root for gratitude also relates to the words gratis and grace, i.e. gratia and gratus, both of which at their roots mean THAT WHICH IS FREELY GIVEN, A FAVOR! Thus, it is directly related to love, which was also touched on in the dialogue, which can only have a meaning that most humans are interested in when it communicates the same thing: that which is freely given!

Sally was perfectly willing to freely give the gift of her gratitude for what had been freely given to her. There is no need for any sense of obligation here, for as noted above, obligation will never bring forth gratitude, but only at best a simple return of what was agreed upon to return or to give. It is an exchange of pragmatic convenience, having nothing to do with love or happiness. We may want that in the practical arena where it builds a sense of stability and reliability. But who wants to nestle with their bank or insurance company or government, Hmmmmmm? So, the real fun of gratitude is its foundation in freedom, like love; in the spontaneity and wonder that humans can generate that most precious acknowledgement from their hearts; that it comes unbidden, which is the quality we revere most highly about being human: that we are free and therefore there is NO certitude in an obligatory, programmed, robotic sense. That we can attend with awe to the appearance from nowhere, literally, of the blossoms of love, gratitude and happiness!

EXERCISE FIVE: FEARLESS AND DEBTLESS!

Alone or with a partner, find the fears and obligations that limit your access to good feelings. Utilize the Option questions as you have understood them from the previous material and exercises. Take plenty of time and listen carefully to yourself or the other person. If alone, write the fear or obligation down and utilize the Option questions to follow the trail your initial statement creates. You may find a delightful surprise in your ability to let go of some of your fears and debts. Any experience of change will be immediately felt. You won't have to search for it. It will be there in your feelings as you move through the process. If working with another, be patient. Sometimes you will achieve a breakthrough and sometimes it will seem to remain unyielding. See how happy you can be with whatever you do achieve. See to what degree you can change your fear to joy and your "debts," should you wish, to a freely given sense of gratitude. Don't stint on really getting into whatever good feelings you do manage to create. They represent your truth and your future.

Chapter Four

Anger/Rage:
The Illusory Antidote for
Fear and the Affirmation
of Righteousness

"PROOF WE ARE 'BAD': All unhappiness is caused by the belief in 'proof' that we shouldn't have been free to have been as we were, which is why we are as we are. The undesirable incident 'proves,' 'shows,' or 'makes it to be' that we are bad for ourselves. The belief that we could in any way be bad for ourselves is unhappiness. Anyone who believes that is, by definition, unhappy.

Anger is believing that they (people) are being made to be against themselves, and it should not have been necessary for it to have happened at this time. They believe that not only are they against themselves, but it was caused by their not admitting or expecting to be disappointed at this time. Anger is feeling wrong for not expecting to be wrong."[9]

One of the things we do when we are afraid is to respond with anger. The classic case of someone creeping up behind someone else and shouting "Booo" usually ends up with the object of that process first perhaps reacting with fright and then, quite possibly, turning from fear into anger, even rage at the perpetrator. One of the experiences that accompanies and defines fear is the sense of helplessness. We feel a loss of control, not only of our feelings, but of our mental acuity and often our physical capabilities. People speak of being "weak in the knees," or being "frozen" with fear.

One way that people strive to overcome their fear is through their anger or rage. This is the "Hollywood" formula so to speak. After being beaten and terrorized, the heroes rise up from the "helplessness" of their fear and are galvanized into purposeful activity through their wrath, their version of "I am sick and tired and I am not going to take this any more!" So it would seem that being angry is a primary way to overcome fear. But does it really? Isn't anger an emotional pain, just like fear. Isn't it true that your anger is not something you would prefer to feel, but either a feeling that just seems to "rise up" in you without your control, or something you feel you must feel in order to experience yourself as socially or morally acceptable. Don't you feel that without the anger either you or the person who may be the object of your anger would not be motivated to do the things that you feel are important to be done or not to be done, as the case may be. Then it might seem that without the anger you would be right back in the situation you don't want to be in: that of being helpless or afraid.

KNOWING, LIKING AND NOT LIKING.

"I am FOR what I am for, and I am AGAINST what I am against, and it cannot be different. In other words, I like (want) what I like, and don't like (want) what I don't like. I can't be wrong. That is just the way it is. Even if I were now to be for what I used to be against, I would still be now for what I am now for, or the converse."[10]

Why do we act? Don't we want what we want? Don't we know what we want? Is the knowledge not enough for us to be moved to go after what we want? For so many humans, wanting has become encrusted with all kinds of impediments and strictures. Cultures and their immediate mediators (communities, tribes, families, educational systems etc.) uniformly mistrust whole categories of wanting because they fear that if people continue to want what they want, then it will be a "dog eat dog" world, people will not be motivated to cooperate in common enterprises for the survival and support of the community, and that basically, people will be wanting things that the culture has ruled bad, evil or things one ought not to want in any case.

So, most people have acquired some fears about what they want, and what it means about them that they might want it. Additionally, mere wanting is insufficient in a world where people feel certain that if they want something and they don't get it, then it will automatically mean they must be unhappy. The distress is not just in the wanting and not getting, but in the sense that accompanies it that that must mean something about them, that somehow they are marked out by the fates, the universe, as "luckless" or "hapless" to use the old English word which essentially means "unable to have HAPpiness! People now speak of "needs", since the urgency of what you want is measured by the sense of expectation/entitlement about having it, and cultures set aside whole classes of wanting as legitimate kinds of wanting described as "needs" so that people will allow themselves to act on their wanting. Now not getting what one "needs" can become the occasion for more fear, the fear of being deprived of something that has been defined as essential for happiness in some way. The prospect of being so deprived can then "kick in" the anger response, i.e., the acceleration of intensity such that one will be motivated in a particularly aroused, and experientially pained way to go after what one wants.

We know the results of anger, don't we. We see the destruction and carnage of its activity all around us. Not that that is in any way "wrong" mind you, but simply stated, it is what it is. People lie, cheat, steal, rape, mutilate, murder singly and by the millions those who somehow get interpreted as standing between them and their "needs," whether it be the mugger who "needs" your money, or the Serb who needs a Bosnian's land or vice versa, or the Nazis who "needed" the cause of "evil" in the world exterminated so that they could achieve their Aryan version of bliss.

All this begins with fear, with the feelings of helplessness and with the radical, assumedly galvanizing response, anger or rage. Now, there are many things in the world we may not like, but so often we may not feel entitled not to like what we don't like. It might mean we were uncaring, or wrong or immoral or being somehow a way we are not supposed to be were we not only to feel okay with not liking what we don't like, but even to revel in the knowledge that we don't like what we don't like. To be happy with not liking is as important a dimension as feeling free to like what we do like. Again, we may fear ourselves for our dislikes, if they contradict the norm of some cultural/social context, and we may act out of that accompanying sense of helplessness to become angry at ourselves for being who we are, and/or at others for judging us unworthy because of our dislikes or our likes. Our contempt for ourselves may grow to such a proportion that it paradoxically manifests in a murderous rage at others whom we hate precisely because they seem to be the way they are supposed to be, while we are feeling hopelessly mired in being helplessly a way we ought not to be. Isn't the cry on the street just before violence is done often: "Now just who the fuck do you think YOU are!" Meaning, how dare you be the way you are supposed to be when I am not. And since I can't stand that you present me with this unbearable contradiction, I am going to beat you or murder you to erase the pain of that agony.

Further, do not the righteous, the fundamentalists of whatever stamp and ideological perspective, require rage against the infidels, the non believers, who by their very existence are an affront to what the righteous see as the truth! Here the paradox of the little childhood ditty I quoted earlier comes to the fore, "Sticks and stones will break my bones but words will never hurt me." Well sticks and stones are liberally used, along with all the evolving high tech capabilities, to break bones, but additionally, WORDS can kill, that is they can get you killed by those who believe in the "voodoo" power of words.

People out of their fears believe that others cause feelings in them against their will. Isn't that how you often experience things yourself? Well then, if simply saying things can create feelings in others, then the rationale for quieting the dissident, by prison or even by death (remember Salmon Rushdie) really makes all the sense in the world, once you believe in the magical power of words to reach in and disturb your equanimity despite what you may say you would want to feel.

So, let it be understood that an Option perspective is in no way the complete acceptance of what is! No, not at all. Nor are we even talking about is the complete acceptance of OURSELVES except in the fundamental sense of knowing that there is never anything about ourselves we have to be unhappy about. There may be things about ourselves we do not like and we can even revel in knowing that and, perhaps, change those things if that is what we want! Therefore, by being happy, we are in no way disempowering ourselves from creating consequences, to the extent we are capable, for others when they do things that we clearly understand to be against the best interests of ourselves or those we love. We may well do this within the frame of the social covenant that we are a member of because we find it in our best interests to uphold that structure, even when it doesn't dispose of pragmatic issues with the dispatch we would want. But, nonetheless, not being enraged, angry or distressed does not strip us of our ability to act on our own behalf. Indeed, I would assert, that through our happiness, we are clearer that vigorous actions on our behalf are perfectly okay because we know we have a complete right to pursue our interests by our own lights, AND we are not burdened by any requirement through our beliefs to hate or be angry at those who would harm us. They are doing what they know to do; we can do likewise in whatever ways we deem best for us to interdict or create the severest consequences for them without a hint of reticence or regret.

EXERCISE SIX: LEARNING TO LIKE NOT LIKING

While it may seem almost irreverent at first to enjoy not liking what you do not like, allow yourself to be open to this notion. Write down, or exchange with a partner as many things as you can think of that you don't like and that you are actually happy you don't like. If you feel stymied to produce something in that category you feel comfortable with, then let me help you by a few generalizations that might serve to prime the pump of your memory and imagination. So, you may be quite happy you don't like the idea of someone mugging you, or of someone stealing your car, or of someone driving a tractor across your flower beds etc.. You see, there are lots of things you are happy to know you don't like! Once you are in the rhythm of this knowledge, then revel in it. Enjoy the freedom to not like and see how it it no way entails that you be unhappy about what you don't like. The clear and unreserved knowledge that you don't like or want what you don't like or want makes any feelings of unhappiness that you might normally be in the habit of associating with not liking completely unnecessary. As you get clear of this kind of association, notice the freedom and relief you feel to share your observations, at least with yourself, without any reservations or sense that by doing so you are being somehow "wrong" or "bad" for yourself.

DIALOGUE TWO: ALLEN'S OUTRAGE

Allen was a young, successful lawyer who came in great distress because his wife had just left him. He was full of tears of anguish alternating with rage at his wife and the situation. He admitted all kinds of sins of neglect of his wife, even though he was a hardworking individual. He really wanted to be a way his wife wanted him to be now, but she had already withdrawn her affections and was adamant that she wanted a new life without him.

He felt helpless, frightened that he could not have what he felt he so desperately needed, the love of this individual, the integrity of his family, the life that, despite his long hours of work and distraction, he felt he had been building all these years. What follows is a crucial portion of some weeks of option dialogues:

F: What about your wife's having left you do you find so painful?

A: What the hell do you mean? Wouldn't you feel pain if your loved one left you?

F: If I did, I would have my own reasons for doing so. What I am asking is what your reasons are for feeling that way.

A: Jesus, isn't it self evident. My god damn wife walked out. I fucked up and now there is no way I can put it all back together. How am I supposed to feel about all that?

F: Even though it may seem that you have no alternative but to feel the way you feel, still, what specifically seems to rankle you the most about your wife's leaving?

A: (now breaking down into tears). Ah shit, I fucked up. She kept telling me that she was unhappy and I kept ignoring what she said. I should have listened, I should have responded and now it is too late!

F: What do you mean when you say "you should have listened?"

A: Just what I said; she gave me warning and I ignored it.

F: When you were ignoring her warnings, as you put it, were you not doing in those moments exactly what you knew to do given all that you understood and believed to be important in those moments?

A: What difference does that make, I should have done otherwise.

F: How could you have done other than what you knew to do?

A: Well, I guess I couldn't have, but still now I feel I should have.

F: To what do you refer when you say you should have, the time when you were actually doing what you were doing, because that's what you knew to do, i.e., ignore her, or now, after the fact when you see the results of your choices at that time?

A: Ah shit, I don't know. Well, I know that I couldn't do anything other than I did, otherwise I would have, I guess, but somehow I still feel now that I should have. Just look at what happened as the result of what I did.

F: So you're saying that if you knew then what you know now then you would have done differently?

A: Yes precisely.

F: But you just got through saying that you didn't know that, otherwise, as you said, you would have done differently. So then what could it mean when you say that you should have done things differently?

A: I guess what I mean is I wish now I had done things differently.

F: But since you didn't why are you unhappy about what you did do?

A: Damn it again, because of what happened from what I did. How many times do I have to say I fucked up!

F: So you are telling me that you love your wife and know that you want her in your life. Then let me ask you this, do you think it would mean anything about you if you were not pained about the loss of your wife from your life?

A: What the hell kind of question is that? If I wasn't in pain then how the fuck would I know she meant anything to me!

F: So then are you saying that your way of making sure that you stay in touch with loving your wife is the degree to which you feel intense pain at her departure from your life?

A: (stops weeping and takes his head from between his hands and looks up more thoughtfully). Say that again, would you.

F: Are you saying that your way of making sure that you know you love your wife is the degree to which you feel pain at her leaving?

A: (considerably more sobered). Well I hadn't thought of it that way. Yes. But isn't that normal. I mean a wife walks out and I'm supposed to feel okay about that?

F: How do you want to feel? Even if you feel pain at her leaving, how would you want to feel if somehow, magically, I could create any feeling in you right now that you want to feel?

A: Well, put that way, yeah, I guess, no, I'm sure I would rather be okay with it.

F: Do you want to create pain to know that you love your wife? Do you not know you love her without the pain? When you first saw your child at birth, was it pain that you felt upon seeing her, or just the pure joy of knowing you loved her?

A: Yeah, no, well, I do. No, I know I love her without the pain.

F: Yes but I sense a hesitation in your voice. Is there any sense at all that to be okay with your wife's leaving would be wrong?

A: Well, it's more that I still find it hard to believe that she doesn't love me anymore.

F: Do you think it means something about you that she doesn't love you?

A: Well, yeah. If I hadn't been such a shithead then maybe she would have still loved me.

F: Are you saying that there is something wrong with you that she doesn't love you?

A: Yes, yes, that's it.

F: But weren't you being just exactly the person you thought you should be during your marriage? And, although it may have turned out to be a mistake from her point of view, weren't you doing what you knew to build a life together, at least as you understood it over those years together?

A: Yes, but it didn't work. All that time at the job, I was too busy being successful and making us financially secure. (Pause, as he ponders that) But, as you helped me see, that's what I thought was important then.

F: And are you saying that now, at this moment, and from now on, which is the only time there is, that you might be wanting to do other than you did in the past?

A: Definitely. I have learned some new values, even if they may not, or will not save my marriage and I intend to live by them.

F: And how does it feel? Are you feeling freer in your gut about your wife's decision?

A: (taking time with an evident clear facial and body expression of growing lightness). Yes. I'm not yet sure that I accept this as okay, but there is no doubt about feeling so much better than an hour ago.

F: And what seems to still hold you back from giving full vent to your good feelings?

A: Well, shit, you know, it isn't as if my wife was all sweetness and light. There were things about her that I didn't like. She always played the role of the victim, the aggrieved party and I always seemed to be the unfeeling, insensitive schmuck. Then she would shut down, shut me out and refuse to discuss things even when I would take the time to pursue what was going on. "It's too late," she would always say, "Now its too late to talk about it and you'll just have to live with having caused me and the children all this distress, as always." And bingo, doors slammed and I'm standing there like a complete asshole.

F: Are you saying that you don't feel okay with not liking about your wife what you don't like?

A: Yeah sort of. You know, I know I fucked up and well, but.....wait. I know that my way of being with her was not conducive to making the kind of marriage she wanted. But I was doing the best I knew to do, given how I was brought up and the values I adhered to. You know, work hard, build a family, be secure. But still I don't feel comfortable with not liking Marie, it's like I'm not supposed to not like her. After all, I'm here crying that I love her, so how can I not like her!

F: Why, if there were and are things about your wife that you definitely did not like, does that mean that you did not or do not love her?

A: You know its funny. I was always afraid to admit, even to myself that I did not like anyone. And in this case, it seemed even more frightening not to like, because I felt it threatened my love for her. But all during those years, I felt I repressed my dislikes and secretly blamed Marie for my not liking her. Isn't that screwy?

F: You mean she was being a way she "ought not to be" and therefore despite her doing from her perspective exactly what she thought was good for her to do and to be, that you were pissed off at her because by being a way she shouldn't be for you, she made it impossible for you to like/love her?

A: Yeah, yeah (smile breaks out). I guess, no I know, I could have shared what I didn't like, or I could have been okay with it. Lord knows there was enough about me she didn't like (more sober now). Yeah, I loved her anyway.

F: Isn't love that which is freely given . And can't you be happy with what you like or don't like and be as loving as you would like in any event? Would you want any other kind of love than that?

A: Not really.

F: So if your wife no longer extends that freely given gift to you, would you want her in any way without that?

A: No, no, I would only want her if she wanted me freely.

F: And is it okay not to like what you don't like, I mean really feel good about that, just as about what you do like?

A: (smiling now). Yes, yes. You bet. It's a terrific feeling!!

F: And how do you feel right now.

A:(broad grin). Damn good. I mean, thanks, thanks so much.

F: You're more than welcome, my friend.

Allen came to accept his wife's decision with equanimity and without judgement; this aided in directing his efforts at supporting and maintaining a good relationship with his children. He ultimately changed his work experience around and made much more space for himself and eventually for another person with whom he set up a more satisfying existence.

EXERCISE SEVEN:
FANNING THE FLAMES OF FEELING GOOD.

By now you have engaged in some of the dialogues and done the exercises and most probably have found at least some spark of change as you examined your beliefs. Perhaps now the opening quote of Chapter One, *The Truth*, may make more sense to you, i.e., that we believe that unhappiness is necessary and that is why we are unhappy; that unhappiness is not getting , or being or doing , or making unhappiness, but SIMPLY BELIEVING that unhappiness is necessary.

But even should you come to know this truth and thereby realize that happiness is the ground of being and is actually all that there is, and unhappiness is the made up illusory state humans have contrived to experience, still remember it is YOUR RESPONSIBILITY to ENJOY your happiness once you begin to experience it. It is through you, your self, your will that happiness comes out from being just a state of relief from unhappiness to a state of active, wondrous joy and even awe and ecstasy.

"The most common unhappiness of people who have benefited by the Option Method is that they regret 'having to' remind themselves. They often deny that because of the way it sounds to them. The usual way that belief is experienced is that 'I should not need to remind myself not to be unhappy. I already learned that.' Why would it be a resentful task to use the most wonderful procedural tool man ever had for being happy, the Option Method? If it is not seen as a privilege to be enjoyed (employed), but if instead is seen as a shameful remedy to a shameful condition, like a medicine or therapy to be endured (ignored), it would be no wonder that they would experience a reverting to some of the old ways.

Enjoy what you learn by employing it at every opportunity![11]

So, start by finding a quiet space and gently focusing upon some small (or hopefully big) good feeling that you either have derived from using this option method or from some area in your life where you can be in touch with a good feeling. Remember, you may have no trouble at all in making the small miseries you experience into more intense discomforts. Indeed, you may wonder about this in a disconsolate sense, that it should seem so easy to do it. That's only because you have been practicing being unhappy from childhood. It is somewhat like preparing endlessly for a big part in a movie that stars "You"; only for some inexplicable reason, before you chanced upon this book, it was a sad, perhaps agonizing , even tragic movie. It is time you realized that you sit in the director's chair and you decide the script, the plot of your own experience of yourself.

Now, you are going to take that capacity to change your feelings (i.e., beliefs) and apply it to the process of ACTIVELY LIVING YOUR HAPPINESS. Sit quietly and let the good feeling, no matter how incipient or apparently ephemeral it may seem to be, rest gently in whatever you understand when I say the "center of yourself." Assume that you are going to feel that good feeling not just now but how it is going to last for at least a minute. Feel confident that that is true and then turn your whole attention to the feeling. Just as if you were making a fire by rubbing two sticks together, the activity of your loving intention to have that feeling be with you will slowly (or quickly) begin to yield some heat and hence some "smoke." Imagine yourself "blowing" on the fire of that good feeling. Go with the feeling that as it grows can last even longer than a minute and keep projecting the feeling out into the future for as long as you wish to keep the feeling alive. If it really takes off, then actively envision it bursting into flames and the flames leaping higher within you so that as you stay with the feeling you begin to soar and the whole of yourself, your entire feeling self becomes filled with the warmth and light of that feeling. Enjoy this for as long as you wish. Repeat it often until your life is aflame with many such fires that can merge into a conflagration of KNOWING THAT ALL IS AND WILL BE WELL BECAUSE YOU KNOW AND INTEND IT TO BE SO, FOREVER, WHICH IS JUST EACH MOMENT AS IT UNFOLDS.

Chapter Five

The Past: Precisely What Can Never Affect the Present

"Let's keep it simple: You have always been what you were supposed to be, and you are now just what you are supposed to be. You have always been allowed to be exactly what you were, and are now allowed to be exactly what you are Whatever you are going to be is what you will be supposed to be."[12]

Being self-reflective creatures, we have the capacity to know our experience and utilize memory and recall to enrich the complexity of our present reality. The weaving of information we have learned into the infinite variety of patterns that can enrich the moment we actually inhabit is a gift of inestimable value. This capacity truly extends our ability to know ourselves and the world and, by ourselves and with others, to combine the raw materials of the universe into entities of endless fascination and practical usage. At the same time, however, humans, as we have seen, coming from their fears have found ways to verify their worst assumptions by utilizing this potentially wonderful capacity of memory and recall.

It is not that there is actually any "past" that exists and which can have any effect on the now; it is past precisely in the sense that it simply no longer is! What actually *is* is simply information we have stored about our individual lives and the people and world around us. This material is not a neutral encoding of information, not some static "encyclopedia" of experiences and events; rather it is a dynamic brew of perspectives and attitudes bound together into belief packages. Therefore, memory does not emerge as if from a book, but rather from the living, acting, believing, hence feeling person, with all the assumptions, presuppositions, that may be part of the interpretive architecture of that particular individual.

49

Our attitudes or life stances have, as we have indicated earlier, emerged from the context of what culture and its servants, state, community, tribe, family etc., have communicated to each new person born and educated in that view of life. So all our versions of what is "good" or "bad" arise from this dynamic cultural environment and we take in, hence accept and come to believe, as a member of that community, in the precepts of this ready made world to whatever degree we do, usually by way of affirming it or by rebelling against it as we grow into adults. But so often even in apparent rebellion we may still feel inwardly bound by the beliefs we rebel against, feeling them to act in us "against our will" as it were. The teenage years particularly, in our culture, are rife with that conflict between outer rebellion and seemingly bold nonconformity along with inner experiences of being torn by guilt over that rebellion. And now, we may feel endlessly enraged by our secret bondage, as we see it, to the very things we may so vociferously denounce in our public presentation of ourselves.

Therefore, the "past" is a creature of interpretation, period! Just look at how historians go about putting together the "truth" about even very recent events. People may agree that events have occurred, i.e. W.W.I, The Holocaust, Communist slaughter of millions, Vietnam etc. etc., but many vigorously disagree over the meaning and value that these events represent, i.e., good, bad, tragic, a hoax etc. etc. Of course, we can indeed know certain "facts" about the past, i.e., that such and such an event did indeed take place. But usually that is not how we utilize this information. Rather we judge, ourselves, others, by what we believe this "fact" of the past represents or means. Thereby does unhappiness arise, not from the innate characteristics of the facts or events themselves, but from our INTERPRETATION of those facts or events. To know this is to know the truth about the nature of the past; not to know this is forever to be in the position of possibly being trapped by our visions of the past, by the pains, agonies, desperations that these events could come to mean to us.

This only adds to the burdens of our mythology of dysphoria, for now we are faced sometimes with having to "recall" events, which we may have repressed out of the belief (perfectly understandable to be sure given the age and the condition of our belief processes) that they were too "terrible" to keep in our awareness, usually not only because of what happened, but more important, what it must mean about US that it happened at all!

Hence every approach is born which in essence simply repeats the shamanistic exorcisms of our ancestors, who believed that demons and devils had the power to enter our very selves and cause us both the pain of their presence and also to act against our very selves by virtue of their power over us.

We give to memories the same causative or, more accurately, pseudo causative power we formerly gave to demons and we require some new kind of "shaman" to exorcise those demon memories by whatever means is currently popular: past lives, pulling it from the musculature or the crystalline structure of the cell, reassociating it from state dependant disassociated fragments of self experience. The expert deals with our conscious self much as the caricature of the old surgeon. We have nothing to do with creating our own wholeness and sense of happiness except to deliver ourselves to the expert who will remove our metaphorical pains as the surgeon would our appendix. Once removed and "sewn up" psychically, so to speak, we can only hope the psychic surgeon "got it all" lest we have to return for endless surgeries to reestablish some shaky semblance of bliss. The language of these approaches may be filled with talk about freedom and self renewal and holistic healing; sometimes people are urged in the midst of the exorcisms to "face the horror directly" in the belief that truly knowing how terrible the terrible thing was will somehow result in one's feeling free. But if "terrible" was and "terrible" can be, then there is no escape from the shadows of the terrible; and, the existential dilemma of being urged to be happy in a world that can at any instant deprive you of that very happiness, even against your will, has got to be the essence of a double bind, if that term is ever to have any meaning. No matter what is stated, the methodology belies the words and the truth is in the reality of what is done.

With Option, the power is in your hands. You have shaped yourself with your beliefs, however you got them from your cultural environment, and you have the power, HERE AND NOW to undergo a mind change, a transformation of your beliefs about the meaning of ANYTHING and hence a change of feeling about that thing.

DIALOGUE THREE: TERRI'S TERRIBLE TRUTH

Terri was a slim, attractive professional person in her thirties who came because of marital discords and what she described a really messed up childhood. She had left a therapy where the therapist had embarked upon a full scale search of her past for physical and sexual abuse. Not that Terri had really repressed any of this. She knew about it and was, from society's standpoint, appropriately upset. But somehow, instinctively, she felt that bringing together all the forlorn figures of the past into a therapeutic "court" where the guilty would be charged and the innocent would have a chance to vent their spleen was not going to change anything about what had happened. She had been through several versions of this before without the results she wanted. She wanted to feel better, not to be vindicated and still live out her life with a sense of having been a victim.

What follows is a dialogue, in the course of many weeks of dialogues, that centered around the past and her experience of salient points of this experience.

F: What is there specifically about your past that upsets you?

T: Well, you know, you have heard me speak of it. I had a stepfather who had his hands all over me when I was in my very early teens and this continued till I fled home at sixteen. And, I had a mother who was forever wringing her hands and entering a mental institution when the whole mess would be brought to her attention. So where should I start?

F: Where does it seem best for you to start?

T: Well, I really feel bad about what happened with my stepfather.

F: What do you mean?

T: You know, I felt dirty and ashamed and angry all the time and there didn't seem to be any way of escaping it or him.

F: If you are telling me that you still feel that way now, then which of the feelings you mentioned seem to be most distressing.

T: Yeah, I guess I still do in many ways. And, I guess, the dirty, ashamed feelings are the worst.

F: In what way do you feel dirty and ashamed over what happened to you.

T: Well, I mean, shit, this guy was hitting on me all the time. I couldn't even do my homework for Christsakes. Why the fuck did he have to latch on to me?

F: What about his choosing you as the object of his physical desires is disturbing to you?

T: Well, come on now. Who needs this overweight, drunken jerk putting his hand in your pants, slobbering and feeling insulted when I would tell him to fuck off?

F: I do hear that you did not want his advances to you in any way. Still why do you feel disturbed that he made them?

T: (becoming angry and animated). Listen, you are damn straight I didn't want his advances. And I didn't do anything to egg him on. Get that straight too. Whatever happened came out of his head, not mine, do you understand!

F: Understood quite well, and therefore, why would you feel upset, or dirty and ashamed at the advances of a man whom you had no desire for in any way?

T: Where did he get off pulling that shit with me in the first place?

F: Are you asking why he was the way that he was?

T: Yes (now becoming more sad than angry). Why couldn't he just have left me alone?

F: Are you saying he was being a way he "ought not" to have been?

T: Sure, that much at least.

F: When we had spoken in earlier dialogues about your mother being a way she shouldn't have been, did you not come to feel a different way when you discovered that she was just being the way she knew to be given her own upbringing and beliefs at each moment of her life?

T: Yeah, I know, that was hard enough, but I could see it and feel it in her case, 'cause she went through a lot of shit like this herself as a kid. But somehow it seems different for him.

F: In what way is your mother being exactly who she knows to be any different from your stepfather being the way he knows to be?

T: Yeah, but damn it he was wrong and his being how he was no excuse.

F: What do you mean "excuse"? Does that mean anything other than you didn't want him to do what he did in any way shape or form?

T: Yeah it means that, okay. But I did not want that to happen; that's what I really mean.

F: Okay, Terri, I understand that, but since it did happen, what about it having happened is so distressing to you?

T: (now sobbing intermittently). I just feel sometimes so to blame as crazy as that sounds for all this having happened, like somehow I should have been more forceful. But, Jesus, things were so chaotic and sometimes even a hug and the promise of affection was better than the uncertainty going on all around, especially when my mother was having one of her "spells" and was so damn unavailable.

F: What about having felt some of his affection to have been comforting is so discomforting to you?

T: Well, it sort of pokes holes in my argument about being so adamant about this guy in the first place.

F: How does liking some of the things that you would like in any event, and not liking the things that you really don't want mean that you really did want what you did not want?

T: (quieter now). Well, I guess it really doesn't have to, but somehow I just can't get past this anger at being stuck with this whole mess.

F: In what way are you stuck?

T: I can't unstick this shit from out of my life. It's like it's just got to go on and on and everyone seems to feel like I've got to be all pissed and agonized over it. I'm just sick and tired of kicking it around again and again.

F: What are you afraid would happen if you were not unhappy about what happened to you with your stepfather?

T: Oh, come on now, how could I do that?

F: I am asking, would it mean anything about you if you were not unhappy about what happened with your stepfather?

T: (silence and a fairly long pause). Hmmmnn. Would it mean anything about me.... Damn, you know, I really truly want to be rid of this thing. But how could it not mean anything about me if I wasn't upset. It would almost seem as if without that upset that I was saying that I didn't have the right to say I didn't want it. Almost like a betrayal of myself somehow. Seems like years and years of investing in the "situation" as we used to call it. Just a lot of people really feeling bad about it, about me, for me. Seems like almost that I would be kind of like "letting them down" you know, as nutty as that sounds
   when I say it.

F: Do you believe that?

T: I don't want to believe that.

F: Then, what would it be like for you to actually feel okay about what happened, especially knowing you didn't want and didn't like what you didn't want and didn't like.

T: (begins to smile cautiously). I do feel better and I do feel more like it would be okay. Carrying that baggage around hasn't done anything for me. Running from what I thought it meant about me put me through two crazy marriages. No, I say it's okay to stop running. I can feel good and hell, I know what I know about what happened. I don't have to feel bad just because others think that is the appropriate way for me to feel. Yeah, it feels good just to be rid of it.

F: Can you really feel that in your gut?

T: No, I'm really there, it's clear and I haven't felt this way since, well since never I guess. It's a new feeling.

Once Terri put to rest the sense that her present reality was in any way controlled by some hypothetical entity known as the past, she quickly put aside major unhappy beliefs about herself, many of which have already been and will be further described in this work. Again check the appendix for an outline of the belief paths in this and other dialogues. We can see these beliefs at work controlling us and feel the sense of liberation as we put them aside. Terri moved to another part of the country and began studies in an area that she had long thought she had not enough intelligence to qualify for. Her progress has been very gratifying to her as she looks forward to an exciting existence free of encumbrances of "past" pains and grievances; she is also living without the dubious, useless mantle of victimhood to burden her free explorations of happiness, a mantle our contemporary social mind seems to value so highly.

SHAME: I AM WRONG FOR BEING WHO I AM, WAS OR MIGHT BE! THE VICTIM SYNDROME.

This belief underpins the shame/victim concept. The "proof" given to the self is that I want what I'm not supposed to want (love, affection, closeness etc.) and out of that wanting perhaps others see me as someone to make the object of their unwelcome wanting. So, that must mean that somehow I am being a way I am not supposed to be, otherwise that person would not choose me. How am I sabotaging myself by manifesting certain thoughts, bodily movements, behaviors? What's wrong with me for enjoying those elements of even unwelcome attention that arise out of my natural capability of feeling warmth and pleasure? How can I avoid being who I am so that I won't "make" other people do things to me that I do not want from them but might well want and enjoy in another context.

This is the apparent paradox/bind that Terri and others with feelings of shame and victimization so often produce in themselves from the initial belief stance that they could ever be "wrong" or "bad" for themselves. We will see the direct follow up of that tendency in the next chapter dealing with trusting ourselves. The freedom, as we learned earlier, to dislike without any accompanying pangs of distress, can empower the Terri's of the world to vigorously pursue those who hurt or brutalize them at any age in whatever way society or circumstances might allow. What is exploded, thereby, is the myth that supports an entire class of "victims," living in varying combinations of painful helplessness and frothing rage. These are people who are encouraged by socio-cultural imperatives to have a boundless sense of outrage that the universe and some of the people who populate it could have the audacity to be a way "they are not supposed to be!" While railing at the completely irreversible and unchangeable realities of what is called the past, they lose precious moments that could be utilized mobilizing their dislike in creative ways, should they so wish, and/or getting on with their lives through the liberation of knowing their happiness in ever more complete and joyous dimensions.

EXERCISE EIGHT: PUTTING THE PAST IN THE PAST

What beliefs have you carried around that you would like to let go of about the past? Make up a list of things you have been carrying around and have come to know you have "had" to feel bad about because you or others believed it was necessary. Use the Option approach to make a thorough examination of the trail of those beliefs. Again, the Appendix might help in this process. Come to really know that you don't have to have any emotional pain from assumptions about whatever happened to you. Get in touch with the earlier elaborated understanding that you can be absolutely free to dislike what you don't like. Note how the intensity of not liking does not have to carry any emotional distress with it. You may even reach a sense of feeling quite happy with yourself for not liking what you don't like and feeling very comfortable with defining yourself by that understanding in this moment. Create a ritual, if you wish, to surround your celebration of letting go.

For example, using the earlier exercise of building good feelings, write down a particular belief that has bound you from the past on a piece of paper. Find a quiet spot and a safe receptacle for burning the paper. Explore the good feelings that will arise from your having let go. Imagine, as in the earlier exercise, that you are aflame with those joyous intensities. As you do this light the piece of paper and concentrate on the process of the flame consuming and transforming your belief from what was apparently solid into smoke and ashes. Feel any sense of victimization dissolve even as your sense of strength through happiness fills your being. Feel the freedom and the wonderful unpredictability of the smoke as it rises up into the open air and join with that sense of lightness to soar and take flight. That belief has become what it always was. Nothing. And now it returns to that state and as the smoke clears, YOU are left, with your good feelings, with your happiness.

Chapter Six

Could I be Bad for Me: Exploring Trusting Yourself

"'Bad for myself" means I am not really wanting for me what I 'should' be wanting for me, and something can prove it. The belief is that this event 'proves' it. Basically, feeling bad means that I believe that what I do, think or want, or feel means I am against my own interests. I believe these are a bad way of doing, thinking, wanting or feeling. The way I am being is a bad (wrong, self-defeating) way of being."[13]

Among the most potent of the fears that we experience is the fear that we could be wrong for ourselves. It arises out of the matrix of cultural concerns that surround us as children. Our parents, relatives, friends, educators all feel duty bound to warn us of propensities in ourselves that may "get us into trouble." So not only do we have to worry about the omnipresent possibility that we will be made unhappy against our will by forces external to ourselves, but additionally, we must be extra vigilant not to somehow succumb to internal seductions and pressures that would separate us from what is right, proper, appropriate and might thereby deprive us of the love and association of significant others. Others who are forever measuring us by our deportment in accordance with the maze of cultural norms, rules, moral imperatives and social mores that are embedded in every waking moment of our life: in what we are told, taught, what we read, take in on television, radio, in all our popular myths, novels, stories, love songs. All are replete with the sour, dour and tragic consequences of veering from the proper path laid out by the world, all ostensibly for our benefit.

It is not strange then that the vast majority of humans find themselves aware at an early stage in their conscious life of not only the supposed "enemy without" but of the perhaps even more pernicious "enemy within": our selves. We have spoken earlier of how that inner turmoil and sense of wrongness can be a pressure cooker that leads many to turn themselves into veritable caricatures of what a particular culture fears. Thus the proliferation of street cultural types, gangs and audacious young people who, out of their often grave frustration with the mass of imperatives that they rail against, opt to become exactly the model of what society doesn't want them to be. It is a paradox that we often become the very thing we fear that we actually may be, simply as a way of relieving the tension of not knowing for sure. Better the certainty of knowing we are "losers" of whatever description (thereby confirm the fears we and others have about ourselves) than continuing to live in the twilight zone of other people's and our own negative expectations of ourselves. This is of course at the core of what others describe as obsessions and compulsions, i.e., the sense of being driven and controlled by errant thoughts in our minds. Merely entertaining these fears is so unacceptable that we must somehow act however irrationally or repeatedly to relieve the intolerable tension we create in our terror of being a way that we are not supposed to be. We end up, perhaps, being just that way to settle the struggle against being that way.

I CAN'T CONTROL MY FEELINGS OR "THE DEVIL MADE ME DO IT!"

It is not only to the young and rebellious that such feelings belong. Indeed, among the most culturally conformist there are ongoing doubts about the worthiness of their own thoughts feelings desires. People are endlessly troubled by fears about their incompetence or how their feelings may somehow "get the better of them." Current headlines shout out version after version of "something just came over me," the modern day equivalent of " the devil made me do it." Because of the fragmented way in which we have come to believe about ourselves, it is difficult to muster anything other than a weak protest, born, perhaps, from some deeper, apparently, walled off intuition, that faintly tells us that this simply is not TRUE!

In a reputed age of Wholism, it is amazing how fragmented and bifurcated we have contrived to make ourselves. Yet, given this experience of estrangement from our very selves, whereby semi-autonomous pieces of what we puzzlingly call our "self" operate in random often, from our belief perspective, dangerously self contradictory fashion, it is no wonder that the belief I COULD BE BAD FOR ME can operate on such a universal scale, thereby making self-trust a perilous choice at best. Now let it be clear that I do not mean "good for me" or "bad for me" in the purely pragmatic sense of what activities and behaviors might best work for me in pursuing what I want. No, I am only talking about the notion that there is anything I could do that could in and of itself, without my consciously making it so, destroy or take away my happiness.

WHAT IF I DON'T GET WHAT I WANT; DOESN'T THAT PROVE I AM NOT GOOD FOR ME?

DIALOGUE FOUR: DOES STEPHANIE KNOW WHAT SHE IS DOING?

Stephanie was a woman in her late forties who now had three grown children and had weathered the storms of what she described as a loveless marriage, at least loveless after whatever initial feelings there may have been. Originally, she had come to piece out the meaning of being in that relationship and she had, through the Option dialogue, come to a place that she considered okay. She was not unhappy and she was exploring many new avenues of self growth and expression with new friends and with an attitude of confidence in that newly found happiness. After a time, I received a call asking for a session. She came in, looking somewhat distracted and proceeded to tell me that she had been diagnosed with ovarian cancer, in a fairly early stage, but nonetheless, she was deeply concerned about her physical well being. She was considering taking alternative routes to treat this illness, and the central issue for her was the question was this alright to do, since so many around her opposed taking a course of action which they considered ill conceived.

F: If you are deciding that this course of action is best for yourself, based on whatever information you have and what you believe that means, then why would you be distressed over making such a choice?

S: Well, Frank, yes I know, I shouldn't be distressed about it but still somehow I am.

F: What do you mean when you say "I shouldn't be distressed about it?"

S: That is, I mean I know that I don't have to be unhappy about this.

F: Then why do you think you would be?

S: There just seems to be something I can't shake about this thing, I mean, that I actually got cancer !

F: What do you mean?

S: Oh, why beat around the bush , I just don't think it's fair.

F: What do you mean?

S: Well, I had just put my life together, a life that had, up to our work together, been mostly a burdensome, bleak existence. So I find I can be happy and boom, a bomb explodes in my world. It just isn't fair!

F: Again, what do you mean by "fair"?

S: Why did it have to happen to me, especially now?

F: What about it happening to you distresses you?

S: Well now I have to make hard choices that I would rather not have to make.

F: Are you saying you would rather not have the opportunity to make choices about your situation, given that it exists?

S: No, of course, I do want to make choices (smiling), I guess I mean I just want the whole thing to go away.

F: Sure, and you know from your work that you could want whatever you might want, but what about its being here distresses you?

S: Well, now that it is here, I guess what I mean by unfair is that I have choices to make and I could be wrong. I mean that could be it, the end, I'm gone if I get it wrong.

F: Let's suppose you do whatever you know to do based on what you believe might work and it turns out it doesn't work. Why would that be the occasion for your unhappiness?

S: Well that would confirm the opinions of others, you know my husband, my daughter, so many friends, that taking this course of action was foolhardy and that I just blew my life on some crackpot therapies, as they term it.

F: Why, even if your way of going about healing yourself does not yield the results you want, would that mean that you were in any way foolish in following what you thought best to do for yourself?

S: (distressed and on the edge of tears now). Oh you see, don't you, I'm so afraid they will turn out to be right and I will be wrong and the result will be my death! (crying now)

F: Which of those things distresses you most, being wrong or the dying?

S: It just seems all my life people have told me how dull witted I was and I often was the butt of jokes, which I myself used to encourage just to ingratiate myself with them. You remember, we talked about this. So now it's like the ultimate confirmation of their opinion of me. Yeah, she's a loser alright. Just look how she handles the most important decision of her life. Its almost like I would be getting what everyone would think I deserve for being so "stupid." My death!

F: Are you saying that you have not explored the approaches you plan to take with all the diligence you know how to bring to this situation?

S: No, no, you know I have really done my homework and I have met some wonderful people who I really believe can help me. Plus all the things I have done for me emotionally and to enhance my physical well being, they all have brought me a whole new world of feeling better in every way.

F: So, then, knowing what you know, in what way could your doing the very best you know to heal yourself be in any way a betrayal of yourself, no matter what the outcome?

S: You know, Frank, I really do feel and understand this on some level, but I can't seem to shake the sense that all these people around me, many of whom seem to want the best for me.... Well I mean, its almost like not following their advice, not really being hopelessly distressed is well, almost crazy somehow!

F: Are you saying it would mean something about you were you not to be distressed in the way people expect you to be about your situation?

S: Yes, that's it. That's the feeling I somehow can't seem to shake.

F: Do you believe that to be happy for you can ever in any circumstance be a "wrong" way for you to be for yourself?

S: No, no I really don't. And especially now, but still there is something.

F: What would that be?

S: I guess its like a fantasy I'm having of dying and all those I left behind nodding their head in a "I told you so" fashion.

F: Are you saying that you believe in an afterlife where your unhappiness would continue and you would continue to feel "wrong" about yourself?

S: No no, you know I don't believe in such a thing. I feel we surrender our individual self and become part of the universe.

F: So, then who is the "I" that is having the fantasy after you die? Through what eyes, ears, neurological functions of any kind are you knowing anything when, according to your understanding, there is no *you* to know anything?

S: (laughing). Yes, that's true. The fantasy is just me here and now making myself unhappy.

F: So how do you feel now?

S: (still chuckling slightly).You know I feel good, don't you?

F: Is that coming from your gut and do you have any reservations at all about feeling good?

S: No, no, none at all. It feels good to know I can only be good for me in my happiness. I'll pursue this alternative approach and give it my all. What more could I ask of myself? In the end, there will be me and my happiness isn't that true?

F: What do you believe?

S: That's what I know.

F: That's right, then, enjoy knowing it.

Stephanie did " follow her bliss" to borrow a phrase from Joseph Campbell's description of the process, and the result in this instance was success. That is, up to this writing, her efforts (it has been four years now) have borne fruit and she is well with no signs of her cancer. Now, of course, the point is NOT that one approach to healing is the approach of choice for everyone. No, the point is exactly the opposite. Whatever you choose is what you choose. There is no way you can be wrong, even if death is the result of your choosing. Trusting yourself, again, is KNOW-ING not just believing, but KNOWING that your happiness is solely and utterly your own reality and this has nothing to do with however adept you may or may not be at creating outcomes for yourself that you or others might define as desirable. Such perspectives are just covert expectations or conditions placed on being allowed to be happy; people set them up for themselves and for others to "prove" that they are "worthy" of the happiness they say they want but do not feel entitled to have UNLESS their activities, strategies, engagements with life of any kind, "prove" by being successful that they are/were "right". Then, they may give permission to feel the good feelings they presumably have no right to feel, would be CRAZY to feel without that successful outcome!

THIS IS IMPORTANT because to know this is to open up a universe of happiness for yourself. But, of course, it doesn't mean in any way that not to know it would also mean anything about you, so relax in any case.

But you might want to join in the next exercise and see what if feels like to be a nut!

EXERCISE NINE: I'M JUST A HAPPY NUT!

Let's have some fun. Isn't that what we are here for? Isn't the world our playground? Remember, the word illusions comes from the Latin meaning "False playing." When we rid ourselves of our illusions, our unhappy conceptions about the world, we can then stop "playing falsely" and then just PLAY. This exercise is inspired of course by my own nutty, wonderful experience of being happy, but also, it reflects in some ways the whole tradition of the "fool" who often wasn't so much foolish, as acting the fool so as to be able to say things that others would not tolerate without that perception of foolishness to protect the "foolish" from the wrath of the mighty. Such things exist in the traditions of the East, but I am particularly aware of the Christian tradition of Eastern Orthodoxy, where in Greek the *salos* or in Russian the *iurodivy* was one who offered some version of happiness through their surface "nuttiness". This is also true to some extent in the ecstasy of the Jewish, Hasidic *zaddikim* as well as in certain elements of the Islamic dervish tradition. We can also think of the "foolish" wisdom of Lear's fool along with the whole medieval and Renaissance tradition of court jesters in Europe and Great Britain. The point here is not mere historical review, but the understanding that to be happy is to be free of the prejudices of those who are all too willing to mark any kind of deviation from culturally accepted expressions of happiness as "nuttiness" or "foolishness" which is a way to quell such potentially "dangerous" manifestations before we all run "amok", infected with terminal bliss!

This exercise can be done alone, with a friend or with a whole group of people. The idea is first to identify all the illusions, all the unhappy, false playing that goes on around us. Take a newspaper, or a series of love songs or a tape of the nightly news, or a sitcom and gather around. If alone as you scan the paper or listen to the song (best on tape) or the taped TV show, stop at the first "false play" you hear. Write it down and consider whether it would be okay for you not to be unhappy about whatever the situation is that is described in print or on tape. Remember, this is not to be confused with liking or not liking. You may indeed not like much of what you experience going on around you, but you don't need to feel unhappy about that. Let us be clear here. No one is asking you to be happy about things you really don't like. We are talking about being happy *even though* there are many things going on that you don't like or want in any way. When you come to really feel joy about not being unhappy about that just shout out "I'm a happy nut!"

Now if you are in a group, it can really get hilarious. All can listen, identify the belief and the one that feels the freedom in their gut to be a "nut" can shout out "I'm a happy nut!" Make it a time limited game with someone counting up the number of "nutty" affirmations for each player and acting as referee in terms of deciding who has raised their hand first upon identifying an unhappy belief. You can also use a timer, let's say, to give each person a maximum of several minutes (the amount of time is arbitrary) to arrive at the gut feeling of being totally okay with being a happy nut.

Naturally, the one with the most nutty affirmations of happiness in the face of all our surrounding beliefs of unhappiness "wins" the title of THE HAPPIEST NUT. He/she gets to keep all the happiness they have created for themselves out of playing the game.....THE GAME IS LIFE, FOLKS, ENJOY!

Chapter Seven

I Really Don't Want to Do What I Am Doing

"People say things like (and feel accordingly): 'I don't want to go to work, but I have to.' The truth is the opposite. You don't have to go to work but you want to. The reasons you believe you HAVE to are actually the reasons you want to.

'We all do things we don't want to do. It's part of life.' The truth is that nobody does anything they don't want to do. All things considered, they'd rather do whatever it is than not do it. Life is only doing what you choose. The rest is what happens. You are psychologically incapable of choosing or consenting to do something you don't want to do....As long as you don't lie by believing that you were lying to yourself you will see what you really feel and want, and how you always act for what you are for."[14]

One of the most common complaints humans make is the one that says, "I don't want to do this." They say this even as they do whatever it is that they are doing. This is also usually accompanied by sighs, moans and other bodily and verbal signs that they are discomforted by doing what they are doing. For some their unhappiness grows apace so that they then come under the heading of being "under stress." People point to the environment, the job, the boss, the guy's wife, his kids, etc., etc., all as "stress" factors in his life that are somehow "causing" him to have high blood pressure, an irritable bowel and high cholesterol.

By now we can see an emerging understanding of how these pseudo-causal relationships are attributed because no one is clear enough to really see that we are the sole arbiters of how we are going to experience ourselves, not our fellow humans or any aspect of the environment, i.e., "Life is only doing what you choose. The rest is what happens." In the next dialogue, we will explore, thanks to Ronnie, some of the dimensions that this assumption of "I don't want to do what I am doing" can take.

DIALOGUE FIVE: SO, RONNIE, GET A LIFE WILL YA!

Ronnie was a tall, stocky young man of about twenty one; he came from an Italian family that was a bit better than middle class and had managed to move out of the "old neighborhood" to a somewhat better suburban setting. While his older brothers had begun to make their mark in the world according to their parents' expectations, Ronnie, the youngest, seemed, both to himself and to his parents, to be mired in adolescent immobility. His mannerisms, dress, speech, all seemed to proclaim that he did not want any part of the "hard work, nose to the grindstone" version of life that had been exemplified in his father's modest rise to prominence as a local lawyer/politician. He had come through a college counselor who recommended that Ronnie see me, since he was dropping out of school and faced an unwelcoming atmosphere at home because of this "precipitous" action on his part. Ronnie felt squeezed. He had the attitude of angry cynicism that manifested in a highly critical joking manner, all of which hid his basic fear of being judged inadequate, wrong, purposeless, and a loser by friends and family. Yet, he could immediately become very engaging and was obviously wanting a way out of his unhappiness.

F: So, Ronnie, how can I help you?

R: Well, Joe, up at college, said that you help people with their unhappiness, so I guess I'm looking for a little bit of that help.

F: What are you unhappy about?

R: A bunch of stuff, girls, a job, my father, but most of all I just really feel down. It's a feeling I've lived with for a number of years now and it's really sticking in my gut at the moment.

F: What specifically are you feeling down about?

R: Well, you know, I dropped out of school and my parents, particularly my dad, is super pissed at me; there's tension all the time and like I just sit in my room sometimes wanting to punch the walls, I get so torn up about this business of being a loser.

F: Do you believe you are a loser?

R: (smiling). Yeah, I know, I shouldn't think that way, hah.

F: I'm not sure what "shouldn't" might mean, but do you?

R: Well yes and no. That is, sometimes I say "fuck you all you people," but like, inside, I feel really bad about being in the situation I am in, like a big, good for nothing pile of shit feeling.

F: What about being in the situation you are in is so painful?

R: Well (smiling again) there it is. My friends are doing well in school, looking forward to med school, law school, corporate jobs, you know really moving ahead. My brothers are like burning up the world with their success and here is Ronnie broken down by the side of the road with his finger up his ass. I mean, I'm like a real *cafone*, you know, a jerk. You're Italian right?

F: Yes, I know what that means, but even if all around you seem to be doing well according to their understanding, why are you unhappy with what you are doing now?

R: Well that's it, right. I'm doing exactly nothing now. I'm supposed to be looking for a job, but everything's slow so I haven't had any luck and my dad says he's not going to help me because I don't deserve his help. So it's like nowhere'sville for me at this time.

F: So, again, even though people around you, are highly critical of you and your decisions about life, why are you distressed by that?

R: Geese, I don't know other than what I just said. I mean the bad feelings just seem right there in the middle of all this crap.

F: And what are you afraid it would mean about you if you were not upset or unhappy about being who you are in the situation you are in?

R: (real pause as Ronnie hunches over onto the nearby desk and focuses himself on what he has heard, smiles). Hey, that's like a lawyer's question, you know, like my brother Al would say. But I got the drift of it. Yeah. You know, so shit, I don't feel bad? Come on.

F: Is bad how you want to feel?

R: Where would I get off not feeling bad about it?

F: If somehow magically I could make you feel any way that you would want to feel about it, then how would you want to feel?

R: (Smiles). You mean like Prozac or something? Well, look, if I could feel a way that I wanted to feel then yeah, who wants to feel like shit?

F: Do You think it would mean anything about you were you to feel okay about yourself even in the face of the disapproval of others then?

R: Well, it's like I said, where would I get off feeling okay about this, with everyone upset and everything?

F: Are you saying that somehow you wouldn't be an "okay guy" if you didn't feel bad about yourself?

R: Right, right, kinda like a real uncaring character not to be concerned about what others feel, you know?

F: So, are you saying that your way of making sure that you are not an uncaring character that doesn't give a shit about other people, is to create all the pain of feeling down about the situation you are in?

R: (stops with his face set in a look of surprised introspection). I never had that put to me that way before. So, yeah, I do feel kinda like I have to be in a shit place with myself. When I'm in my room that's one of the things that really gets me pissed, is like who proclaimed me the "designated loser" of this family. It's like "Ronnie's role" since day one, you know.

F: Do you want to feel those bad, down feelings then?

R: To be honest no, I don't.

F: So what would it be like, right now where you are sitting to let them go and feel differently? Can you go inside and test that out?

R: Feel good about it? So…(he looks up to the ceiling and leans back in the chair as if in search of some sense of himself inside and after a bit responds, smiling). Holy shit! I did actually feel different about it. Yeah, but right now as I am saying it, I kinda lost it.

F: So go back and get it.

R: (takes some more time). Son of a bitch. I got it back again(smiles). So, yeah I could be okay with that.

F: You really feel that way in your gut, is that true?

R: Yeah, I'm being straight. I didn't think that's what was going to happen when you asked me but, baboom, then there it was (smiles and laughs a bit).

F: Great, just take a moment to really revel in feeling and knowing that.

R: (spends some time). Hey, this is okay, I mean, this is new and it's okay.

F: So, then, how do you feel now about the situation you were describing a moment ago?

R: Better, much better. I guess what bugs me now is more my dad. You know I just can't be anyway that's good for that man. I mean I can't stand to be in the room with him, sometimes I hate him to the point of exploding, you know?

F: What about the way your Dad is with you is so exasperating?

R: What's the big deal, I mean. So, suppose I don't want to be a lawyer like Al or a doctor like Vinnie. So fucking what (turns red in the face) he's got to treat me like a dirtbag because I'm a little confused right now about things? I mean fuck him, that's what!

F: Are you saying your father is being a way he ought not to be and that by doing so he is making himself a way that you can't love him so that's why you hate him?

R: Fuck, that's another lawyer's question, but yeah, you are right, who the fuck is he to be who he is?

F: Is he not being just the way he knows to be, given his upbringing, his beliefs and feelings as he applies them to each moment that he lives?

R: (taking his time, thoughtfully with the question) Ah ha. Yeah, so I guess he is, but fuck him anyway!

F: Are you saying that you don't like him?

R: (smiles) Yeah, you might say that's a reasonable conclusion from what I just said.

F: And is it okay not to like your father for being ways that you don't want him to be?

R: (radical change in emotion, turns slightly away with eyes downcast and welling up with tears) Ah shit, yeah, I mean no, I mean why the fuck doesn't he like me. I mean I really do want the guy to love me. What the fuck is so bad about me anyhow, tell me that?

F: Ronnie, I am sure that you do want him to love you and accept you in the ways that you want that; but if your father, with his reasons for being the way he knows to be, can't extend that kind of love or caring to you now, what about that is so painful?

R: It's like I said, I wonder what the hell is lacking in me that he doesn't like me?

F: Why do believe it means anything about you that, again, given the way your father believes and feels, that he doesn't like you?

R: (composing himself and straightening up in the chair) Ah hell, guess what, you're right. He's the way he is and I tried my best to be his fair haired son, but I guess the slots were already filled by Al and Vinnie.

F: And if you were not upset about this, what do you think that would mean?

R: (pauses but for a moment). Hey (smiling), I'm hip to it already. I guess I feel if I don't get all bent out of shape that means I don't love him and won't try to change his mind about me.

F: And how do you feel now about that, about him?

R: Better, better. Yeah, it's good. I didn't think coming in here that any of this would happen, but yeah I'm definitely in a better place with this whole thing.

F: So is there anything else?

R: (smiling broadly now). Hey, Francesco, you got a job for me?

F: No, but why do you ask?

R: 'Cause I sure hate what I am doing now, you know, a little bartending, a little construction, mostly a little nothing. I guess what's left is that I really don't want to do the petty shit that I am doing now. It bugs me that my friends are all positioning themselves for the kill in life and I am embarrassed to even run into them now.

F: Well, what do you mean when you say that you don't want to do what you are doing now?

R: Hey, like I said, it's bullshit work. I don't like it and I don't want to do it.

F: Well, you just got through clarifying that it's okay not to like what you don't like, but don't you have your own reasons for doing what you are doing now?

R: Sure, of course, I don't want to hold up in my room with my father in the house. So it's good to at least be out during the day, or at night, even in the bar; at least it's work, so that it doesn't look like I'm rotting on the street corner with my lowlife friends.

F: So, then in doing what you are doing you are serving your own purposes at this time, isn't that true?

R: True, so?

F: Why do you think you have to be unhappy about that by saying that you don't want to do what you say you have good reasons to do?

R: Well, because I don't want to do it, that's why.

F: And what are you afraid would happen if you were not unhappy about doing what you are doing at the present?

R: (Pause again, then smiles broadly) Ahhhhh, Yeah, the same old shit again. That's right. It's like if I was okay with it, then I just like sit in it and not do shit about it. You know, like I got to bitch and moan to keep myself aware that this is not my life's vocation, right. Shit, I don't want to do that.

F: So then why do you think you would?

R: Well, I don't, I mean I won't.

F: Is it okay to be happy and still not like what you are doing and know that you prefer to do other things and will pursue doing them in the best way you know how?

R: (smiling). Yeah, sure. It's not even that I'm really so bummed out by what I am doing. It's like I'm "supposed to be" 'cause it's like not "worthy" of me, like my mother puts out at dinner.

F: How are you feeling about what you are doing?

R: Hey, Francesco, it's cool, I'm okay. I don't really have a direction right now but, you know, I just really like hanging out and reading serious stuff, Dostoevsky, Tolstoy, you know the heavy weights. I don't know where that gets me, but hell it's what I like.

F: And is it okay to not know your direction right now and at the same time be happy as you explore whatever possibilities come up in your life?

R: You got it. That's the truth. And I feel it. Thanks.

F: Ciao bella Ronnie. Enjoy.

Everyone will be happy to know that eventually Ronnie got a job; that job enabled him to return to school locally and pursue studies in Russian Literature, a strange vocation for an Italian boy from New York, but an adventure of a lifetime for Ronnie.

HANGING OUT WITH WHAT YOU WANT: LETTING GO OF CONDITIONS ON YOUR LOVING, SO THAT THERE IS NO "IF YOU LOVED ME YOU WOULD BE THE WAY YOU ARE SUP-POSED TO BE SO THAT I COULD LOVE YOU."

From this dialogue we can observe some things we already know about the legitimacy of liking and not liking and how that is different from the pain of anger or hating. We can see again that true compassion is knowing people are doing the best they can AND knowing this in no way disempowers us from pursuing what we want with vigor. We don't have to be burdened with feeling bad about the way people perceive us or want us to be. We can let them have their vision of us and still love them even when we don't like them. We can certainly feel totally free to act on our own understanding of our best interests even when that brings responses of outrage and indignation from others who "know better" than we what is "good" for us. So the issue of self-trust, again, gets exposed for the true nature of what we could come to know it means: that I cannot be "bad" or "wrong" for me, meaning that I have to be unhappy about what I am doing or about the outcomes of my efforts in the world.

Ronnie could let his father be who he is and surrender the pain of hate; he could let HIMSELF be who he is and surrender the pain of self-loathing and he could be happy with whatever it makes sense for him to do at any given moment and surrender the pain of doubt about his motivation to go after what he wants in life. Loving is just another word for Happiness which is just another word for Freedom. In several dialogues you have seen and will see the question of meaning of either our or another's love. What we could know is that we truly value others freely giving their love to us. Loving derives from xaris in Greek, caritas in Latin, all of which means a gift, that which is freely given. So often we may find ourselves in situations with people where we fear the loss of their love, when, as we explore our beliefs, we clearly see that what we call love is not at all what these people are offering, but only their version of love conditioned by all kinds of expectations and demands deriving from their beliefs of unhappiness.

Knowing that, we can revel in our freedom to offer our gift of love to another who might be freely and unconditionally welcoming of it and willing out of their loving freedom to return their own reciprocal gift of love; but that in no way means that we do not want what we want in a relationship. We are perfectly free to pursue our preferences as to how we want to be related to and what conditions we will find congenial to remaining in a relationship. In short we are free to love whomever we please, however we please, whether they are the way we want them to be or not; whether their love for us is relatively unconditional or laden with conditions. SINCE OUR LOVING IS OUR FREE GIFT, IT IS NOBODY'S BUSINESS BUT OUR OWN WHOM WE BESTOW IT UPON OR FOR WHAT REASONS WE MIGHT DO SO. Thus,

Ronnie can, by letting go of his demand that his father be any particular way, dispense with hate and allow his loving if that's what he wants, no matter how his father might not be willing to reciprocate. That in no way means he is surrendering his desire that his father be the way he wants him to be. It just means he doesn't demand/require it for his own happiness, that's all. That's the wonder of love. No one can stop you from loving them, no matter how they may despise you or reject you. Your love is the joy of your happiness and, as has been so often repeated, you can never be wrong for doing what you do. SO, LOVE WHOM YOU PLEASE, AS OFTEN AS YOU PLEASE, IN WHATEVER WAY YOU PLEASE. ENJOY YOUR LOVE!

EXERCISE TEN: LOVING THE YOU THAT IS DOING WHAT-EVER IT IS DOING!

See how wonderful it can feel to be really okay with whatever you do. Only if you believe there is some agenda you need to accomplish in order to be happy will you hold on to your misery about what you do in the moment, as a kind of "pledge" to somehow force you to "get to" what you "really" want to do. Only when you attain that, or do what you say you must do will you allow yourself any happiness. To do otherwise would be endangering your stated motivation to get out of this "shitty" situation that you don't like.

Again, take a piece of paper, or gather with a friend and review what you are actually doing and how you feel about it. If alone, write out your hopes and desires for yourself, all the things you would love to have in your life. Now focus on what you are doing and if alone, use the Option questions in the spirit of the dialogue to follow your belief trail. See how much of your discomfort and unhappiness you can trace to the fear of feeling okay about your present activities, lest it sap your resolve to get to some other place. As you are able to surrender those feelings and become more and more comfortable with your present life, then turn your attention to the things that you desire to do. Notice how, without the pain of fearing you won't have what you say you MUST have, you can range with ease and pleasure over all the items that seem attractive to you and truly feel good about wanting those things. Free from the tension of anxiety over not having them, see how they take on a different light and meaning for you. See what dimensions of those things become clearer or change. You may be even quite delighted to find that without the obsessive or compulsive quality to your wants, that some of them simply disappear and anything that really appeals to you remains. There may be a wonderful rearrangement of your wants and desires in the absence of the pain of believing that you don't want to do what you are doing, because admitting that you do want to do what you do now bears no ill promise of making you in any way less intense about pursuing a greater and deeper understanding of what you might be wanting in the future.

Chapter Eight

There Must be Something Wrong with Me

"Deep down inside I have something wrong with me. I'm 'crazy'. The fact that we would, of course, fear this, shows how evidently untrue it has to be. Why would I fear my deep self-destructive urge toward unhappiness if that was in me? How could it disguise itself as a desire? Simply, the concept is full of internal contradictions. I could only fear self-defeatingness out of a desire to avoid self-defeatingness; just as I feared unhappiness because of my desire to avoid unhappiness. Is not that desire from my selfishness which I should not trust. What shall I then trust? My fearful distrust and my suspicions of my selfish desires would still have to be a manifestation of that inherently selfish desire to protect myself from the punishment of greater unhappiness."[15]

By now many of you will be seeing a commonality to all unhappiness. There is the appearance of complexity to unhappiness much like a formidable tangle of shoelaces that dissolves into the simplicity of a single string with a tug on one end. This network of appearances are the beliefs that block you from ever getting below that surface level of presuppositions to the what I call in another book, *The Unbearable Wrongness of Being*, primal dread or basic fear. Thus all the manifestations of unhappiness really are generated out of one simple equation: we are unhappy because we believe, i.e., are afraid, we have to be, period. From this the patterns of misery spread out in every direction and encumber and interpenetrate every quantum of human experience. The landscape of distress seems without any horizon or limit. The more it is explored without knowing that primal assumption, the more mysterious, convoluted, improbable and impenetrable are both the reasons that humans contrive to explain unhappiness and the solutions they derive to deal with it.

So exploring some aspects of how unhappiness manifests is on the one hand never to exhaust the reasons people give themselves to be unhappy, and on the other to illustrate that it is by far unnecessary to address all the categories of human unhappiness so as to somehow "prove" the application of the Option Method to each one. Each human is an individual and individually experiences his/her unhappiness in his/her own way. The Option approach simply accompanies that person as he/she explores a particular mode of being unhappy. We have seen already, that the few Option questions, in all the variants they may be asked can deconstruct any human construct called unhappiness, given the willingness/capacity of a given human to engage in that method. And the ability to do so comes first and foremost out of the ATTITUDE of being happy and secondarily out of the applied art of asking these questions over and over again in the context of doing the dialogues. To paraphrase an old Latin saying "Option deals with what is human, and nothing that is human is alien to Option."

DIALOGUE SIX: WHY IS MARTY NOT A MENSCH?

Marty was a reasonably successful physician in his early forties who had been married, divorced and now was out in the "singles" scene and felt overwhelmed by what parents, friends and the world seemed to expect of him. That was that he should find an appropriate mate, have children (the first marriage had no children) and just in general be a "mensch," that is, in various interpretations, a version of a macho, potent, woman loving, children generating family man who would fulfill the vision of that concept in the eyes of others.

Not finding himself pursuing the course that the culture had laid out for him, he began consulting experts who in turn began to explore, in his past, present etc., a whole host of reasons why Marty was indeed not a

mensch. There was, according to them, a plethora of developmental, unconscious, archetypal causes, along with in one case, Marty's just plain "orneriness" that kept him from seeking true intimacy, that made him impotent in bed, that indicated his repressed homosexual longings. Marty came to consult me at the time when a systems therapist was arranging a choreographed corrective experience with several generations of what the therapist termed his entire dysfunctional family. His presentation was basically that he knew he was a schmuck (if he sounds like Woody Allen, he wasn't, but physically, he was not altogether dissimilar in appearance and mannerisms) but nothing could be done; nonetheless he had heard that I had some approach having to do with being happy and what the hell, a little happiness couldn't hurt (this was followed by a kind of self deprecating nervous laugh). Despite his sad sack presentation, or better said, as a kind of defense against his beliefs about himself, Marty had a kind of standup comedy routine that he did by way of making fun of himself in that Woody Allenish kind of comic tradition.

F: Marty, what makes you believe that there is something wrong with you?

M: Me, wrong with me? Nothing, no broads, no erections, no orgasms, early to bed, early
to rise. What could be wrong with me?

F: Are you saying that there are things, experiences in your life that are so self-evident as proof there is something wrong with you, that you find the question to be absurd?

M: What, how? You should have a few of these things wrong with you and you would be asking such a question?

F: If I had any of those experiences I would deal with them in whatever way I see fit, but why are you unhappy if they are what you experience?

M: Listen, Doc, I came here for a little bit of happiness, not to discover my therapist is psychotic.

F: In what way is asking you about the reasons why you would feel distressed by what you experience mean I am crazy?

M: Well, okay, so maybe you're not crazy, but you're the first shrink that didn't take my situation for granted that I was *meshugah* (i.e., crazy) in some way for feeling what I felt.

F: Why do you feel *meshugah* by virtue of having the experiences you have described?

M: What can I say? First, it doesn't feel good not to feel good, and secondly everyone else thinks I'm a wimp. From this I'm supposed to feel good?

F: However you may actually feel, what is there specifically about what is going on that
distresses you?

M: You want specifics? So I'll give you specifics. My mother calls me up every day, in the middle of patients, whatever. If I was in the operating room with a gallbladder in my hand someone would hand me a portable phone and it would be my mother saying: "So Marty when are you going to bring home a nice Jewish girl. What, there aren't good nurses there at the hospital. You want to die all alone like your Uncle Phil with all the urine all over him and no one around to make him decent?"

F: What about your mother's constant badgering of you to find a mate upsets you?

M: Hey what am I supposed to do, wear a sign around my neck. Enough already! Where's it written I have to find a woman and settle down. Tell me that!

F: I don't know Marty. Do you believe that because your mother or anyone else wants your life to be a particular way, that therefore you must make up your life according to their formula?

M: So, now you're telling me I shouldn't settle down?

F: I'm asking you whether you believe that because others have a scenario set out for your life that somehow you must follow it to be happy?

M: Oh Doc, you are on to a big one there. Like humongous. I can feel centuries of tradition, all the rabbis dressed in black carrying the scrolls and wagging their fingers at me: "So Marty, you know better than all of us, ha. Somehow your puny little brain knows more than all the laws and the prophets, so if Marty doesn't want to settle down, fine. Just ignore three thousand years, the pleas of your ancestors, your mother. Go, have a good time in the world. Don't give us any children. Just go, be happy, ignore all those who really care about you."

F: And die like your Uncle Phil with the urine all over?

M: (breaks up laughing, we both break up). Yeah that's right Doc. Hey you got it. You're sure you're not Jewish?

F: Okay, Marty, but do you really believe that. That is if you don't conform to what others have scripted for you, no matter what their motivations may be by their own understanding, that somehow that means something about you?

M: (considerably more sober in mood now). Ah (rubbing his hands through his hair) I don't know. You know, the first marriage was mostly arranged. Everything was in place the way it was supposed to be, but, what can I say. There just was no chemistry. She was a nice girl and everything, but when it came right down to it, I just didn't have any feelings for her, I mean no feelings, get what I am saying here. Ohh, I felt so bad for her, so guilty. What a mess, getting out of that. Such pain, such *tsuris* (pain, trouble). Who needs this. To hell with my ancestors. They should be in such a position. (pauses). Come to think of it, they probably were (starts to smile). So, where does it all end, hmmm.

F: What are you wanting Marty?

M: Me, want? Marty should want? Did Marty want to be a doctor? Did Marty even want to go to Yeshiva? Does Marty want to go to the bathroom? What does Marty want?

F: That's what I am asking you. What does Marty want?

M: Is there an echo in here? I feel like we are doing a comedy routine.

F: Would you prefer not to be asked questions about your unhappiness?

M: No, no, I'm just screwing around. It's just that I have not even really thought in terms of what Marty wants.

F: Are you saying that thinking about what you want would pose a difficulty for you?

M: Is that not obvious? Who am I to want?

F: What do you mean?

M: Well, where I come from wanting can get you into trouble. You might not want the right thing and even if its the right thing you might not want it in the right way. And even if you want it in the right way you might not get it anyhow, so why bother to want it in the first place.

F: Are you saying that if you don't get what you want that you have to be unhappy about that?

M: Well, why bother wanting if you don't really want what you want?

F: Are you saying that if you were not unhappy about not getting what you want then it would mean that you didn't really want it?

M: Hey unhappiness and not getting what you want go together like peanut butter and jelly, you can't conceive of one without the other.

F: Are you saying that your way of making sure that you really want what you want is to create the pain of unhappiness to make sure that you know you really want it?

M: (pause). Ah, ah, ah. Interesting. Okay, so I can see that. What do you know, that does make sense. Hey, Doc, you know you are going to be very unpopular with my ancestors. But yeah.

F: How do you feel?

M: Well, better, but what about all the rest of the shit, the erections, the orgasms, my Uncle Phil?

F: What about them?

M: It still doesn't feel okay to feel okay about not feeling okay about them. Hey Doc, I'm beginning to sound like you, No?

F: What are you afraid would happen if you were not feeling unhappy about the things you mentioned?

M: The word *meshugah* does come to mind. I can again just see all my ancestors moaning and groaning about how Marty doesn't really care about anything.

F: In what way would your not being unhappy about these things indicate that you did not care?

M: Naw, you know, it wouldn't really mean that, but there is still some sense of it not being quite right.

F: How do you mean?

M: Well, if I am not unhappy about these things, why would I do anything about them? I mean seriously now, I know that I kid around a lot, especially to take the focus off myself, I guess. But, I really do want to have a better life and, in my own way and time, a relationship with someone. So how do I know I am going to do that? I mean truly, it is amazing, I do feel better now, but what does that do for the future?

F: What do you mean by the "future."

M: What Doc, you don't know from the future? You don't know to put out your garbage next Thursday? You don't know from mortgage payments due next month? Boy the bank must love you!

F: I mean do you live in any other moment but the moment that you actually experience?

M: No, I can just handle one moment at a time, that's true.

F: So when you say "future" are you really talking about anything other than some thought you are having now, even though you may speak of a thing called next month or next Thursday?

M: So good, that's true, so what?

F: Then how do you feel now, I mean right now?

M: Ah ha, now. So now I feel good, okay.

F: Is there any other moment for you to feel okay other than the now that you are in?

M: (quite sober). No, this is it and now, fair to say, I feel better than okay, my ancestors not withstanding.

F: Feeling good now the way you do, is it your intention to continue to feel that way, even as we speak, even as the last few moments have evolved, do you continue to feel good?

M: All true, true. I do want to feel good.

F: Then why would you believe that you would not continue to feel good, every moment, each moment at a time?

M: Oh well, a moment at a time I can feel good. But who lives a moment at a time? (laughs) Just kidding Doc, I got it. The answer is everyone, right. But suppose I forget to be happy?

F: Suppose that you do. Won't you be delighted to remember, should that occur, that you can indeed be happy?

M: Ah yes. That's true. It's like discovering your happiness all over again. I guess I would even feel better, knowing I never really have to be without it. How's that Doc. Did that all by myself.

F: So, do you still have trepidations that your happiness won't last?

M: No, not at this time, and as you said, my mother should pardon you, this time is all that there is.

F: So, how do you feel Marty?

M: So good, terrific. So why are you always bothering me with all these questions about my unhappiness. Who asked you anyway? (We both break up laughing).

A GOOD LAUGH COULDN'T HURT!

Marty continued to prosper in his dialogues, and we both continued to laugh at his humor, a humor that gradually began to lose its self-deprecatory tone, but not its sense of identifying the anomalies, as he came to see them, of life and how people make themselves unhappy. It was a humor that came from a gut clear of negative assumptions about happiness. This can be one of the most ecstatic joys of feeling good. It is like a great generator of sympathetic waves that coaxes into resonance every fiber of your being. You know how wonderful your gut feels after you have allowed true unconditional mirth to wash over you like a warm cleansing spring rain. So, when you are allowing of it, LAUGH. Think of Marty, and break yourself up!

Several things stand out in this dialogue. First, Marty, like so many unhappy people ultimately, believed there must be something wrong with him. While he joked about it, it was a great source of anguish. How could he stand against the world, his world, centuries of tradition, the opinions of experts and assert his happiness in the face of all that? Didn't he have to be a certain way to be okay? After all, he had "problems" and weren't these clear signs that there was something wrong with him?

Second, even if he could be happy, there is the ongoing experience of the mysterious transience of happiness. Remember, most of us believe that unhappiness comes unbidden, against our wills so to speak. So even if you feel good in a moment, you could lose that equanimity no matter what you personally wanted. This is the myth that Marty deconstructed at the end. Let us also remember, again: THERE IS NOTHING "WRONG" WITH BEING UNHAPPY. People are doing the best they can with what they believe and there is no ideological imperative to be happy! The "happy police" are not going to come and take you away for being unhappy! This is not about constructing just another straitjacket for humans to wear, the straitjacket of HAVING to be happy. No. What we are talking about is the GOOD NEWS. The good news that happiness is available to all, to you if that is what you come to by virtue of KNOW-ING that happiness is all that there is and unhappiness is merely the belief in having to be unhappy. There are no "have to's," "shoulds or musts," attached to being happy. That is precisely what happiness is NOT! So any-one who preaches, teaches that there is a way that you have to be or must not be in ORDER to be happy is by that fact not talking about, cannot be talking about what I mean by happiness: that is THE UNCONDI-TIONAL PERMISSION TO THE SELF TO BE FREE AND THE FREEDOM TO BE HAPPY WITHOUT CONDITIONS OF ANY KIND! THAT IS THE GREAT DEMOCRACY OF BEING, OF ALL THAT THERE IS, THE ACCESS FOR ALL WITHOUT REQUI-SITES OR RESTRICTIONS OF ANY KIND TO BE HAPPY SIMPLY BY BEING SO. IF YOU WILL, THIS IS THE DIVINE GIFT RESI-

DENT IN EVERYONE OF US SHOULD WE DISCOVER IT! HOW
THE FUTURE CONTROLS THE PRESENT, NOT THE PAST

*"People feel now what they believe they are going to feel in the future. They feel whatever feelings they believe will 'happen' to them. They feel now whatever they believe it will be 'natural' to feel in the future, even if it is as a result of something happening now. The current event correlates to current emotions only insofar as it relates to imagined future feelings. These feelings, whether assumed as natural, inevitable, or just going to happen, are simply other ways of expressing the belief that they are necessary; which belief is the real cause of the feelings."*16

And so, happiness is NOW because now is all there is, no matter how we contrive in our fantasies to speak of the past or future as actual realities. I dare anyone to give me a million dollars NOW next Thursday; or to give it to me NOW last Friday. Yes, it does sound absurd. But that is essentially what we do when we are unhappy about the past or when we dread the future (By the way, in the spirit of Marty, all are free to give me a million dollars now, that is whenever the now is that is now for you). So, the question of losing our happiness is an illusion again, since we would then have to be believing NOW that some past or future event could deprive us of our good feelings. That would only be felt NOW, even though we might be talking of some event next week. This opens another important understanding, i.e., it is not the past that we use to create feelings in the present, but always the future. Even when we experience things which we identify as past, we are unhappy about them only as we believe they will affect us now or in the future! Naturally, then, all unhappiness is the assumption that no matter what we feel now(like Marty's I'm okay now but what of tomorrow), there will come a time when we will feel unhappy against our wills, and that will be so either because mysterious forces external or internal to us conspire to create the feelings, and/or we feel we must feel unhappy otherwise we would not be decent human beings (what would Marty's mother think of you?).

EXERCISE ELEVEN: LETTING GO OF MARTY'S MOTHER

Hopefully by now you are a "nut" in the spirit of the earlier exercise. Exercise your vibrant talents as a true happy nut and tease out for yourself any beliefs that resonate with Marty's presented dilemmas. Again, if doing this alone, write your beliefs down on a piece of paper and use the Option questions to follow the trail of your beliefs. If with a friend, do a dialogue, patiently, like an authentic happy nut, and with as much of that freewheeling sense of open nuttiness, known as the Attitude, as you can muster.

In any way do you believe that there is something wrong with you? Write down what's "wrong." When you have made your list or communicated it to your partner, then explore why, even if things are not the way you want, in light of whatever is "wrong", i.e., symptoms, some personal or interpersonally identified shortcoming, you still cannot experience yourself as okay with that. See the degree to which you may still believe in the MYTH OF PERFECTION, i.e., the notion that you are not worthy of being happy (because that would take away your motivation to do anything about the things you may genuinely want to change) until you have somehow actually "achieved" what you want. Remember, happiness delayed, is happiness denied, is just plain unhappiness. The notion, again, that it would be wrong for you to feel good, I mean really deeply, profoundly terrific, before being a way that you and the world believe you must be to be happy, is just the sadness of believing in the inevitability of unhappiness. In a PERFECT world (according to the definition of the unhappy) no one could ever possibly be happy! In a HAPPY world (one where you let go of the myth of unhappiness and thus affirm your happiness) everything is PERFECT, JUST AS IT IS! This by the way says nothing about not LIKING the way things may be. You may not like ANYTHING about the way things are, and still know that has nothing to do with your happiness. To be stuck in a dungeon by a repressive regime or to live in some kind of narrow fundamentalist society might well be things you really would not like. Less extreme might be your rela-

tionship with your family, friends, boss, the lack of financial success, your
state of health etc.. But, the joy is in knowing and experiencing that even
there, no matter where, you don't have to be unhappy about that. There
is a play called "Fire on the Ice" which depicts a relationship between an
older concentration camp inmate and a newer young man, living in
Arctic conditions, no food, eating rats out of the latrine, faced with
instant death from camp guards at any moment. Yet, the younger man
finds the older man to be upbeat, indeed happy. So he asks him: "Tell me,
how can you be happy here in this place under these conditions?" The
older man looks at him and after a pause replies with a smile: "Tell me,
where else is there for me now to be happy but where I am. And here is
where I am. If you have a better place to be happy in, let me know and I
will gladly accompany you forthwith!"

As you do this exercise and go from item to item, sense how deeply you
can rely on your KNOWING what you want as you come to know it. If
there are things you truly want to change, then don't you know that?
What purpose is your pain? To make sure you know what you already
know? No, it is there because, in the language of earlier chapters, you
believe you could be "wrong" or "bad" for you and you affirm thereby the
corollary belief of this chapter, "therefore there must be something wrong
with me!"

Then, when hopefully you have achieved a little or a lot of equanimity
about some or all of the items, ask yourself, do I have any sense at all that
my present good feelings about this are subject to change against my will
at some future time? Reread the part of the dialogue about the present
moment. Do you now understand being in the moment you are in? If you
do just shout out "I'm a nut" which means in Option speak, Yes. As you
get clear about the permanence of your good feelings, how they are totally
under your control, then revel in the feelings, roll around in them, as you
would in the surf or in the grass on an open meadow or on the rug.
Indeed, along, with a friend, or with a group, just roll around on the rug,
beach, meadow, bed, giggle, laugh and shout how great it is to be a "nut"

to be happy.

"Perfect."

Everything is what it must be.

There is nothing wrong. Everything is precisely and exactly how it should be. Everything that is now has come necessarily from what caused it. Freedom to Change the Perfect.

You may change or wish to change anything that is. There is nothing wrong in that either. That is perfect"[17]

Chapter Nine

The "Big" Ones: Guilt, God, Judging and Death!

All the themes that we have dealt with have, if you have been reading closely, repeated themselves. So that, as mentioned earlier, unhappiness is layered like an onion with many overlapping leaves which, when finally unfolded, leave nothing at the core. Therefore, there is no need to categorize and deal with every human "ill" in some clinical way. To repeat, each individual experiences his/her unhappiness uniquely, but the answer to the unhappiness is always the same: it simply is knowing that, no matter what the given circumstances, we merely believe in it and we can let go of that belief. In this chapter, then, we are going to highlight some issues that most people identify as "core" to the potential for human unhappiness. We have, in various ways, as you review our previous dialogues, already dealt with them, but the person whom I will be presenting over the next pages, offers an opportunity to examine them from yet another individual's perspective. We shall plumb some of the specific implications following the dialogue.

DIALOGUE SEVEN: MONIQUE'S AFFAIR WITH GOD AND DEATH.

Monique was a very attractive black professional woman in her early thirties who was dealing with her feelings of difficulty over her marriage of some ten years. She felt herself in many ways to be dynamic and assertive, a kind of "in your face" person as she sometimes put it. At the same time, she was afraid of what she called her "submissive" side, a side that had for her overtones of mystery and danger. She had been referred by someone who had profited from the Option Method, but she was wary and skeptical of what this approach could do for her.

As we worked over a period of weeks, she brought to light some aspects of her life for which she had experienced shame and dread. It seems that her father had been involved with her in some sexual manner and, as in the earlier dialogue with Terri, she carried a good deal of guilt over that experience. As she let go of the beliefs that she had to feel bad over what happened, she then came to a period after the birth of her first child when things in the marriage were really in "an angry, crazy place," in her words. During that period, she had an affair with a co-worker which was brief, but which disturbed the image she had of herself as someone who "did not do that kind of thing." She began to have grave doubts over her self-control and her ability to stay committed to the relationship. Also, she made the "mistake" as she put it, of confiding in her husband's cousin, a woman she had known since childhood, but who over the course of the marriage, after this time, became increasingly distant and hostile to her. At the time of this dialogue, Monique is talking about the affair and her fear that her cousin might decide to tell her husband about it, after all these years, and what that might mean for her future.

F: Are you saying that you still feel unhappy over having had the affair?

M: No, well, I'm not so much unhappy about that, I mean, I can see what I was about doing at that time, although then it really felt that somehow this man had some strange power over me.

F: Do you still believe that he had some power over you?

M: No, from our work about my father, I feel much clearer that I was just believing that in some way I didn't have any right to say no, especially since I was feeling so abandoned at the time. No, its more now my feeling that the exposure of the affair would really upset Curtis. You know, he's his father's son and there's not much room for straying from the straight and narrow with those folks.

F: Suppose that Curtis were to learn about the affair, what about that would be upsetting for you?

M: Oh man, righteous Curtis. I can just see him in my face with all kinds of "I should have known's," and "My mother told me so's."

F: Yes, and if he is really upset, still why would you be distressed about that?

M: Well, hell, I weathered the storm of those early years. It wasn't easy and I still don't have any Bill Cosby scenario at home. But it's been better than it was and there are some really good moments. I just don't want that witch tossing a bomb in my life.

F: I do understand that you don't want that, but if that were to occur, why specifically would that be the occasion for your unhappiness?

M: Damn it, Curtis is an "old school" type of individual, despite all those natty three piece suits and liberal talk. His woman in bed with some other guy. No way.

F: What do you mean?

M: I mean that that might well mean the end of our marriage, that's what I mean.

F: And if that were to be the case?

M: That would be a real kick in the butt, that's what.

F: What do you mean?

M: All that trying and "being good" for Curtis down the toilet because I let somebody get in my pants during a tough time in my life. Life just doesn't give you any slack.

F: How do you mean that?

M: Like I said, I'm not worth anything to this man unless I'm his "good little girl" so to speak. Now that may sound like a contradiction, given the way I present myself, but that's what it's like in the bedroom.

F: Are you saying that if Curtis were to decide on the basis of your having had an affair that he no longer loved you that that would be a cause for your pain?

M: (looking sad and depressed). Yeah, that's what I'm saying. Miss "new woman" is just a plain old "scairdy cat" under all that gloss.

F: And are you saying that the kind of love that Curtis would display under those conditions, a love that could not see beyond the notion of your being unfaithful in that time of stress, that that would be a love you would find worth having and feeling pained about losing?

M: (taking some time to chew that over). Well, you know, its a lot like what we talked about with my father, isn't it. He was the most distant unreachable man as I knew him as an adult and it took me till I met you before I could just cut him loose and know that whatever he did and however I tried, there was just no way I could make that man love me, the way I wanted him to love me. So, I guess, here we are again. Damn, if I could get past it with my father, then I know I can get past it with Curtis.

F: What are you saying?

M: I don't want no love from someone that would be so damn stingy with it that they couldn't extend some understanding for my situation years ago. Hell, I don't even know if he will ever know, but I'm not going to live under any sword of Damocles with this man. If the witch tells, hell, let her tell. If that busts his bubble, then good riddance. It's not like Curtis is some paradigm of virtue.

F: What do you mean?

M: There are lots of things about him that I am not pleased about, just plain don't like and it even has eaten me up to feel that I don't like him sometimes.

F: Why is that?

M: Same old crap. I just wanted and want things to be "perfect," whatever the hell that is. I couldn't stand myself because I was so vile as to betray him and I guess I can't stand him sometimes because he is the way that he is.

F: Are you saying that he is being a way that he ought not to be?

M: Yeah, well, damn I guess so. Yeah and I know that that's how I experienced myself until I could let go of judging myself, but sometimes I feel just who the hell is he to be so high and mighty?

F: Are you saying you hate him for being a way that makes it impossible for you to love him?

M: Yeah, sort of, no that's it.

F: How else can he be but the way that he is given what he believes and feels?

M: Yeah, I know, even as you were saying it. He can't. I mean I have been the way I have been, given what I felt and believed, so how is he supposed to be some other way than he is? Yeah, judging him is bullshit; he's just being his old Curtis self and I am just moaning about "po me" for having picked him again.

F: So how do you feel?

M: Now, well now I'm feeling lots better.

F: Do you still feel in any way that you have to judge him, even though you may not like him?

M: No, I'm in a better place with that, but I still bear some grievance in my heart for his father.

F: What do you mean?

M: You know. There he is dying of cancer and everyone expecting me to be supportive of Curtis, to say nothing of being caring for that old stiff necked hypocrite.

F: What do you mean?

M: Hell, I don't feel really free not to act like something terrible is going on, and I guess something terrible is.

F: What terrible thing is going on?

M: That man's dying is what's terrible. You know the way he is going I don't wish that on anyone, dried up old codger that he is. He won't listen to anyone about what ways there might be to get some real help for the cancer and I dread the kind of pain he will be dealing with. I saw it with my mother and it wasn't pretty.

F: Why, even if Curtis' father will not listen and may die a very painful death, is that a terrible thing?

M: How is his dying not a terrible thing?

F: Why do you believe that it is?

M: How am I supposed to believe it is not?

F: What are you afraid you would happen if you were not to believe that his dying was terrible?

M: Oh, that question again. Okay, well, its like before, what kind of person would I be not to feel terrible at this man's dying, dislike him as I may?

F: So, are you saying that your way of maintaining your sense of being a decent, caring individual is to agree that this man's dying is a terrible thing?

M: Yup. I got it. But the man still is going to die hard.

F: Won't he die just the way he lived, in the best way he knows to do it, given all he has believed about himself and the world?

M: Yes, true, he will. But it puts me in mind of my constant prayer to God.

F: What's that?

M: God, please, whatever you do, don't take me like you took Momma and leave my two girls without the softness of a mother's touch. I must admit, if there is a fear of death, then it's for those two sweet things, not so much for me.

F: And if you were to die and they were to face life without you, why would that be distressing or painful for you?

M: (tearing up a little). God has no need of me and those two loves want their Momma, that's all I know.

F: Listen, Monique, since you believe so strongly in a loving God and an afterlife, let me ask you this, is it possible for God to be unhappy?

M: (pauses for a bit to think). No, no. God can't be unhappy. God is bliss, so that is for sure.

F: And could God in any way intend for you or anyone for that matter to be unhappy?

M: No, that wouldn't be in God's nature. Quite the opposite as I would understand it.

F: So, if you were to die and your children were not to know their mother, would that in any way imply that God wanted or desired you or them to be in any way unhappy about that?

M: No, I guess that's true. God couldn't want that.

F: And if you were with God in heaven as you understand that, is there any way possible that you could be unhappy, even given the fact that your children would be facing life without their mother?

M: (pause and then responds). No, no. When I think of it the way that you ask it, there would be no way.

F: And no matter what kind of life your children might come to know on this earth, would not all come to happiness with God at some point?

M: Yes, yes it unmistakably would, I believe.

F: So doesn't God know that all is okay, that all always was okay and all can never really be anything but okay, even if humans contrive to envisage their existence in quite a contrary way?

M: I do feel that now. That is God's perspective.

F: And isn't God happiness, if either the word God or happiness is to have any meaning at all?

M: (smiling broadly now). Okay Mr.Happy Man I'm definitely with you now.

F: So, then how do you feel, any doubts or reservations about your happiness?

M: Nope, I am at peace. Thanks.

F: Enjoy your happiness.

Monique continued in her marriage and continued to feel better and better about herself. She reported to me that her change in Attitude had attracted her husband's attention and that somehow he was now much more flexible and attentive than before. She felt more confident in the quality of their feelings for one another and let go of any feeling of being threatened by what anyone else might reveal about her past.

GUILT, JUDGING, HATRED

"Guilt is feeling bad for not feeling bad when I should. It is believing that I will feel bad for not having felt bad, or for not having believed something would make me unhappy. It is feeling bad for 'making' someone else feel bad instead of me. It is feeling bad for making or allowing myself to feel good when I should not have felt good."[18]

We can see from the previous dialogue once more the repeated patterns of unhappiness, especially in guilt and in judging self and others. It can be quite clear that guilt is just another byproduct of believing that we could be bad for ourselves. Feeling the pangs of guilt or trying to make others feel those pangs is presumed to be the way to "control" our otherwise errant and perverse wants and longings, so that we will not act on wants we should not want and thereby not be a way we "ought not" to be.

"It follows, of course, that since we can believe about ourselves that we should be different, we can and will believe it about others. To believe that another needs to be, or should be, different is judging another, and simply an expression of our being unhappy."[19]

Should the internal restraints of guilt fail us, despite the pangs, then of course we are open to being judged by others or by ourselves. It is as we have seen, judging is the appraisal of someone as being a way they ought not to be. In that state of being a way they ought not to be, they, we assert, deprive us of the ability, the "right" even, to love them. And, it is but a short leap, one heartily encouraged by the righteous, from judgement to hatred, which is simply a more intense pain of experiencing this sense of others "being wrong for being who they are" and thereby our presumed reflexive response of the painful dislike called hatred.

"If you believe that something can cause your unhappiness, that is fear, and loathing of it."[20]

Under the hatred, for some, there may be the ever present sadness of "having to" again feel a way we would prefer not to feel, but perhaps do not dare not to feel lest we thereby mark ourselves out as "patsys" or "insufficiently politically correct" or "aligning ourselves with the immoral and the degenerate or the heretical." Thereby we may risk drawing upon ourselves the opprobrium of the community (religion, family, spouse, friends etc.) of those that may demand the hate!

GOD AND OPTION

"Ecclesiastes
3:12 'I know for sure that there is absolutely nothing better for them than being happy and making the best life for themselves.
3:13 This includes each and every person: Eat and drink, and see how truly good are all your efforts—this is a gift from God.

Translation from the Hebrew by Bruce M. Di Marsico"

In this dialogue and the earlier one with Stephanie mention was made of death, the afterlife or lack of it, and of God. What Option is about is happiness and, therefore, what I offer to those who would want to learn about themselves and their happiness is that truth alone: that happiness is what is and all that there is. Therefore, there is no contradiction at all in accepting Stephanie's version of what death means to her and simply following the logic of her fears to the point where she feels comfortable surrendering them and taking possession of her equanimity. Equally so with Monique, whose vision of death and God and an afterlife was explored because she made reference to it as part of something that she was interpreting as a reason she had to withhold her access to her own happiness.

Therefore, there is no Option dogma about how one is supposed to conceive of these notions. The central point is only the degree to which in any way they might be used as a reason to be unhappy, no matter under what exalted banner of all that might be purported to be lofty or meaningful. So, if in following the logic of anyone's beliefs, one finds that person coming to liberate his/herself from any bonds to some unhappiness, then it is in no way incumbent upon the Option practitioner to attempt in any way to disabuse that person of what he/she may hold as true about what they call God or death. Nothing is nor ever could be at stake in what people believe about such things, unless, of course, they make it the occasion for their distress.

For you could come to know, there is no hierarchy of experts and anointed ones who hold the arcane rituals of salvation in trust for only the worthy to attain. Your happiness is a fait accompli. It is like living the life of a pauper while your bank account is bulging with riches. You just don't believe you are wealthy, you are not supposed to be, it would be wrong for you to be, so you never really dare to check your balance. But all are. If some actually are making use of their riches, it is not so as somehow to "affront" others. Rather it is a beacon of hope that by example proclaims: this too is YOUR birthright, not because any guru gives it to you or any required "path" defines it for you, but because it simply is!

And so there is the decision to know without exception or reservation that unhappiness is merely the choice to be unhappy and that happiness is what is left for you to affirm and enjoy when you change your mind about that choice! Indeed Happiness is not the choice, for once happy there is no truth to annul that reality; you don't then have to choose happiness but rather employ or enjoy it in your life. Only by your choosing unhappiness, by believing in the contingency or dependence of your happiness, can you in any way place yourself into illusion again, thereby playing false with yourself. Thus, what you do from moment to moment is to choose in that moment NOT to believe whatever belief you might become aware of as engendering your unhappiness. What you actually experience by so doing is the relief of that surrender, and what is THERE without your having to do anything about it is YOUR HAPPINESS. It is there because it is the very ground of your being, not something you bring into being by choice. It was always there in some fundamental ontological sense simply waiting to be enjoyed. You had actually to CHOOSE to deny it, through all the interactions of your earliest moments in life, in order to dissociate from its existence as the fundamental fact of YOUR existence.

The image that I like to use is that of a beach ball floating upon the surface of the water. If you leave it alone, then that is where it will stay. That is your happiness. In order to submerge the ball beneath the surface(i.e., choose to be unhappy), you actually have to expend a great deal of energy to forcibly keep the ball underneath the water. That is why unhappiness seems so often to be draining, enervating, fatiguing because of the energy expended to maintain the illusions of unhappiness. Then, when you release the ball, what happens? It naturally floats back to its primal position of happiness on the surface of the water. How you use your "ball of happiness" is of course your business in living out the infinite possibilities to know your joy and equanimity. Therefore, when you stop choosing to be unhappy, by whatever you believe, there your happiness stands, arms outstretched in eternal welcome, ready to usher you into a universe of awe and wonder without end. So Happiness is what is. Unhappiness is the Choice!

THE MOST DIRECT METHOD FOR KNOWING YOUR HAPPINESS

Here I am going to quote from my other work *The Unbearable Wrongness of Being* in which I paraphrase the Option Founder's direct method for knowing your happiness. It goes as follows:

"You could not make up being happy. What we call believing we are happy is merely reflecting the truth of our happiness. If you don't want to feel bad, then under what circumstances would you continue to feel bad? Only when feeling bad will stop you from feeling bad! Feeling bad is seen as being honest and therefore admitting you feel bad is a way of making sure you can't fool yourself, so that you won't believe something that is not true, i.e., that you might believe you feel happy when you might actually be feeling bad! Ask yourself the following questions as the ultimate shortcut to being and maintaining your happiness:

DO YOU WANT TO FEEL BAD NOW?
IF NOT, THEN DO YOU WANT TO BE HAPPY NOW?
IF YES, THEN NOW DECIDE IF WHAT YOU JUST
SAID IS TRUE! YES?
THEN BE HAPPY, MY FRIEND!"

Having said that then, and in the spirit of the serious whimsy that being happy generates, I invite you into the great Democracy of "happy nuts," the fraternity/sorority of all who are equal in having access to their happiness, a world where all are their own experts and gurus and none is ever any "better" (a word that would derive from being unhappy anyhow)than anyone else simply because they are happy. We are happy because we want to be and that just simply makes us congruent with the truth of being, of what truly is, that is, our happiness. That's it! So Good for Us, as my client Marty might say. Let us be in true awe of our happiness and, out of that freedom, that Attitude of Complete Self Assurance and Independence, perhaps, we will spontaneously experience giving ourselves the gift of gratitude. For the Option Method is not the herald of any Salvation, for Salvation is not at hand....it was never out of our hands. We merely believed otherwise all these millennia. So, there is no one to save, nothing to fix, no great conflagration or upheaval to endure. There is just the eternal now, which has always been, is now, and will always eternally be now. And, there is YOU being happy as you see fit to be so! Gee, what might come of that?

EXERCISE TWELVE:
EXPERIENCE YOUR HAPPINESS WITHIN YOU

As with all the other exercises, this one can be done alone or with others. As always choose the most congenial context in which to do the exercise. Now on paper or with a friend, review your beliefs about God, Death, Judging or Guilt. See how in any way they may seem to demand your unhappiness as a price for your allegiance to any particular system or tradition of religious beliefs. Reflect on what has been said about the nature of God. Would God want your pain, suffering or discomfort? For what reason? What has God, Who is Happiness, to do with how humans contrive to make a "hell" of their existence. Come to know that any such "hell" is an illusion.

As you come to really feel there is nothing to impede your access to God, to your Happiness, then let the "Spirit" of God, your *pneuma*, be your own breath and exhale all the falsehoods your beliefs about God and pain and suffering and guilt and judging may represent. Make it long and deep and feel it right down to the floor of your gut. Then inhale, inhale deeply the Spirit of Happiness, the Spirit that is the Universe, all who dwell within, you yourself, and the God that is your Happiness. Truly feel that YOUR OWN UNDERSTANDING OF GOD IS WITHIN YOU AND IT IS YOUR HAPPINESS!

Chapter Ten

The Case of the
Purloined Perfection

"Happiness is being glad for who you are:
liking that you want what you want,
liking that you don't like what you don't like,
liking that you change your mind whenever you think that's best,
liking that you don't change your mind until you really change your mind,
liking that you don't like not knowing how to have what you want,
liking that you don't like being mistaken,
liking that you feel just the way you like to feel about everything you do, and
liking that you feel just the way you like to feel about everything that happens.
Everything is the way it is, and you really can be glad to feel the way you
do."22

In this our last chapter, there is a tale to tell of a woman who all her life had sought enlightenment; endlessly she journeyed and trained with all the leading lights of West and East, wherever they were to be found. Still, her happiness escaped her. Finally, she found a guru, a man she came to respect and trust and through her work with him she found herself a close member of his inner circle. This is not some "horror" story about a "bad" guru, for this individual was by all reports kind, well meaning and caring of those who put their trust in him.

Still Loretta agonized over what she considered her defects and short-comings. It was one such dimension of those "defects" that eventually brought her to me, through a mutual acquaintance, sort of through the back door as it were. She came to me in great secrecy, feeling it very urgent that no one know that she was consulting me. What she revealed was that she had over the years had many lovers, and this despite the imperatives of her beliefs and the understanding of her guru that she live a life aloof from such" illusory attractions" of the flesh. Nonetheless, she would always "fall" as she put it, crawl back to seek forgiveness and understanding of her failings, but try as she might, she could not put off her desires for men.

Now, there was an additional dimension to her dilemma, as she understood it, one that reflected the reality of our times very much. She had discovered that she was HIV positive. So, it was not just a matter of shriving herself of her failings, but there was now the undeniable "stain" of her illness that loomed in her mind as a kind of Divine punishment for her faithlessness, even though her guru tried in his own way to assure her that he held no such feelings about her plight. What follows is a salient portion of some of our work together around this issue.

DIALOGUE EIGHT:
LORETTA'S LAMENT FOR PARADISE LOST

F: And so Loretta, how can I help you today?

L: Why does my bliss so elude me, that's the question that just won't go out of my mind.

F: What do you mean?

L: I mean just that. Why after this time and all this effort am I sitting crumpled up here at fifty one with a sense that nothing I have done since I was nineteen has made a damn bit of difference? (starts to weep).

F: What do you think it means?

L: I don't know. How about that nothing makes any damn sense anyhow. How's that for starters?

F: In what way does nothing make any sense for you?

L: Ahh. You know what I mean. All this enlightenment crap. I've been banging my head against the door to bliss for decades. Maybe its time for me to acknowledge that its all just a lot of hype and I'm just too frightened to own up to it.

F: What would you be frightened about?

L: Frightened to learn what I guess I already know. That we are all on our own and no one really knows dickshit about anything. Not really.

F: And what about knowing that, if that's what you should come to know, would be unhappy for you?

L: Why would I like that? That's not what I have been searching to know all these years. It's a bitter pill to see the world that way after having such high hopes.

F: In what way is it painful to see the world the way that it is for you?

L: Come off it. I know you are into your version of *samadhi*, your "happiness" stuff, but who are you anyhow? You've got this crappy little office and a beat up old car out front. And I don't see you up on a dais in front of thousands of followers the way Ramakrishnanda (pseudonym) is. So where do you get off questioning my vision of the world?

F: Are you saying that you don't want me to question your vision of the world? So what are you wanting now?

L: (softening a bit now). Hey, look, its not like I want to insult you or hurt your feelings. Ann did say that she really felt a true radical shift in her experience by coming to you. And knowing the dead end place she felt herself in, I really have to respect that. I guess, it's just that I've sort of been "to them all" so to speak, and somehow I don't get the sense that whatever you do you are knocking the world dead.

F: Are you saying that despite what your friend has told you you know you can't be helped and especially by someone with a beat up old car who doesn't have the adulation of thousands? So then why do you think you would seek me out at all?

L: (half grinning, puckishly). Can I say its a measure of my desperation? (turning serious immediately) I guess you can see how profoundly cynical I am about everything and (bursting into tears again) I am so ashamed of how my life has turned out, how utterly powerless I actually do feel to do anything about it (sobs deeply for a while).

F: Sure, I do see, hear and feel that you are profoundly unhappy. What about your life, however you may not like the way it turned out, is something you feel ashamed about?

L: God, you would think *something* would have come of all those years. I mean, I was sincere, worked hard at the disciplines I studied, but nothing seemed to "take." There's always been an emptiness, a kind of gnawing sense that whatever others around me may be getting, that I was out of the loop on that experience.

F: Do you believe it means something about you that you did not "get it" in all those instances?

L: Well, Christ, I'm not a stone. How am I supposed to feel when the years slip by and each successive "path" turns out to be a dead end, at least for me. How am I supposed to see this as a good thing?

F: What are you afraid would happen if you did?

L: How's that?

F: What are you afraid would happen if you in fact did see your life as okay in spite of all the things you did not like or want about it?

L:Hmmmm, so okay, that would be a ridiculous thing to do.

F: What do you mean?

L: How would it help me to lose the "edge" of my awareness of how distasteful things have become for me. I mean that's not enlightenment, that's stupidity to become "numb" to one's life and existence like that.

F: Are you saying that your way of making sure that you continue to know that you don't like how your life is going is to cause yourself this deep despair so that you will not be indifferent to it?

L: Well, I don't know about deep despair, well, yeah, you're right, that's what the hell it amounts to. But the discomfort, now I don't know. Even Ramakrishnanda teaches that there are moments of terror and despair and one has to keep a deep awareness of these things else one never finds a way to any state of bliss. Hmmmm, yes there is a fear of letting go of that "edge" I was describing, but, yeah, I can begin to touch what your question implies. Like, God forbid I shouldn't lament my life, especially now when we are not just talking enlightenment but a slow and painful death (tears well up).

F: What about letting go of that "edge" would be so fearful?

L: (still tearful but thoughtful and taking time to respond). You know as I range over my life, all my attempts to somehow shake this anguish that seems to have "stalked" me since early childhood, it's almost like I kind of knew in advance nothing was going to work and the only comforting thing that I really knew was always there, and this is going to sound crazy even to me as I say it, but it was the lament, I mean the bitching and moaning; like each successive failure had its reward of giving me the perfect right to raise my fist to heaven and cry "foul" and damn it let no one dare say nay to me on that. That was mine, is mine and (now beginning to cry more deeply and speaking with difficulty) Jesus it's become all I have. Imagine that, my fucking pain, for Christ's sake. You know, I feel so shitty and ashamed right now I just feel I have got to get up and go (begins to shuffle in her chair as if to leave).

F: Of course you are more than free to do that if you wish, but perhaps before you go you might just entertain one more question. What would it be like for you, here and now, if only for an instant to surrender that lament and see what you might come to experience without it?

L: (still leaning forward in her chair as if on the edge of leaving). Okay, that's a good question, but I don't know if I can do that, I mean, I don't think I ever really have.

F: Sure, but what would it be like just to go inside and see if that might be possible?

L:(pausing and slowly letting go of her "edge of the chair" posture to relax back into it and then responding wistfully as if in meditation). Yes, you know its like a space, an emptiness a sense of nothing?

F: And if you were to go along further with that where do you get to?

L: (more time and introspection and still with "far away" tone in voice). Still more nothing, just space and nothing. That's it.

F: And how does that "space" and that "nothing" feel?

L: How does it feel?

F: Yes, how does it feel to feel what you have been afraid to feel all your life?

L: (long pause and almost stunned posture of being frozen in some moment of realization and then finally the puzzlement congeals into a more sober, brighter, almost radiant aspect). Ah ha. Ha, ha, well. Hold on. Yes I'll be damned. You're right (beginning of a smile) you're right. That's what it was. It wasn't pain, it wasn't the lament and the bitching and most of all it wasn't the anguish and the fear. I'll be damned, it was nothing. I could feel nothing!

F: And how does "nothing" feel?

L: (more smiles). A damn site better than lamenting I can tell you that. But wait a minute. Is that it? Nothing? You mean I have been defending myself against literally *nothing* all my life?

F: Are you saying that what you just said about "nothing" feeling good was not what you felt?

L: (look of surprise again) Ahhh, I'm beginning to see something here. Are you saying that the nothing is really a something, like maybe good feelings?

F: What do you believe?

L: Well, shit. It's the first time I have sensed feeling something authentic, something that has really come from myself and not from some act I put on to impress a teacher that I did in fact have whatever experience I was supposed to have. Jesus, that's rich, leave it to me to have good feelings parading around inside as "nothing".

F: How do you feel?

L: Well, as long as I stay in touch with my "nothingness" I seem to be alright (laughs). It's a riot. This is the kind of talk we talk at the ashram, but I always felt it was bullshit. So nothing is not always nothing. That's great!

F: Is there anything else going on?

L: (sober again and on the edge of sadness in demeanor). I guess the word nothing has a double edge to it. I mean its great to finally see a light at the end of the existential tunnel so to speak, but there is a lot of darkness still around for me.

F: What is dark for you now?

L: Well, some of the bitter fruit of all this trying to be "perfect" act I have put on all these years is that I am left with all the guilt of being a phony, a sense of betraying people who I believe really did and do care for me and a legacy of death because I never mastered my physical needs. Now it is here big time right on my doorstep.

F: What among those things that you mention seems most urgent for you to explore?

L: Well, I could start with the guilt, since it seems to cast a shadow on all the rest. I can't seem to forgive myself for essentially deceiving myself as well as others.

F: Are you saying that you were ways in your life that you ought not to have been?

L: Hmmm. Yes, that's right, and somehow I shouldn't have been those ways. After all I knew better, I had studied so much. For God's sake, I could sit for a whole day in Lotus position for a ZaZen experience, or do Yoga like a champ or run weeklong intensive workshops with the utmost intensity and concentration and so on and so on. And people really did say they profited from my work. I have many compliments on what I have done and written, you know that. So where do I get off doing what I did to myself and other people?

F: Did you not say with much passion earlier on in our session that you had been so sincere, had studied so hard, had desired what you call enlightenment with as much intensity as you could muster?

L: Yes, that's true. I said it, and what's more I meant it. That's not bullshit. I know that in my heart.

F: Sure you do. And weren't you, while you were pursuing enlightenment and bending your efforts to know what you wanted to know at each and every moment of all those years of effort, doing the very best you knew how *given what you knew, understood and believed about yourself in the context of each and every moment of your experience?*

L: (pause to chew that over). Yeah, when you put it that way, that's true. Given what I felt and believed, that was my best.

F: Then in what way could you have done other than you have done?

L: No, that's true, I could not have.

F: So if you were doing the best you knew to do and could not therefore have done otherwise, why would you feel guilty or regretful about your experiences?

L: Well, look, okay, maybe I don't have to feel guilty about having done what I have done, but God, look at the consequences for me now! I'm freaking going die from it, that's what! How do I get past that shit?

F: What about the prospect of dying is difficult for you?

L: Ah phooey. Come on. Guilt is one thing, death is something else. We are talking "end of life" stuff now, not just anyone's life but my own (tears begin to appear again).

F: Okay, but, again, what is there about dying that brings painful feelings for you?

L: (weeping and talking). You know, it's right back in the toilet with that feeling of shame again. What an ignominious end. I won't be able to hide it forever and then people will know I have fucked up. All the respect and status, yes god damn it, I admit *status*, will go down the tube. No one knows I slept with someone, and I damnsure can't say I got it from a toilet seat (forced smile). It may be pathetic, but I really covet that place next to Ramakrishnanda. There is at least some warmth and a sense of purpose in being in that place at this point in my life.

F: Going along with your assumption that those people would think less of you for your behaviors, still what about their knowing and disapproving causes you discomfort and shame?

L: I guess it gets back to that same "I should have known better" or "I shouldn't have done it" stuff. But I kind of really do feel clear that I was doing the best I knew how. So I guess its more in "their knowing and dis-approving" that hurts.

F: What about that hurts?

L: Well, there it is plain as shit. I've lost whatever vestige of a life I might have had by my actions, even if I was doing what I knew to do. That won't change the minds of other people about me!

F: And what are you afraid would happen if you were not to be fright-ened of the disapproval of others?

L: (pause and without any tears). Okayyyy. There's that question again. You mean not to give a shit about what others think. Seems like a pre-scription for being alone to me.

F: What do you mean?

L: Well, if you never take other people's views of you into account, how do you expect anyone to grow or know anything about yourself? If you don't care about having people around you then chances are you won't have people around you. Doesn't that make sense?

F: Are you understanding from what I asked that were you not to make sure that you would be *frightened* at the prospect of others disap-proving of you that you would somehow then not care or take steps to engage and involve yourself with others and make a congenial social net-work for yourself?

L: (Pause again and then a kind of lighting up in the face). Shit! Okay, same thing, yes, same thing. The same thing as earlier. Damn, so, it tastes like the business with "nothingness" again. And if nothing turned out to be a something, then what about this?

F: Are you saying you wouldn't know you want human company except if you were pained by the threat of constantly losing it? Do you not know what you know about what you want?

L: Okay, I do know. I know I want people in my life without the pain, but it's a complicated deal up at the ashram. There's more politics than one might suspect and not a few people are already jealous of my position with Ramaj as we call him.

F: Are you saying that you would want the company of someone who would not be accepting of you were he to learn of the ways in which you have lived your life as best you know how?

L: No, you know, I'm not really saying that. I wouldn't want that, but after all the crap I have put out about him, the truth is that he is not a problem and I know he will have no problem accepting me no matter what.

F: So then, what is disturbing you?

L: You know it's not him or them, but me. I just can't forgive myself for bringing all this upon myself, despite all we have talked about.

F: What is there to forgive?

L: You know, the AIDS, particularly that, I guess, remains.

F: Again, when you contracted it, did you set out to do that, or were you simply going after what you wanted, some human warmth and closeness?

L: It was human warmth and closeness to be sure, but God at what price.

F: Are you saying that from the perspective of what you knew then at that moment, or afterwards when you discovered some consequences you did not consider?

L: Afterwards of course.

F: And are you saying that this proves that you are somehow "bad or wrong" for yourself because you should have known what you could not know given what your assumptions were when you acted?

L: (almost smiling). Yeah, that sounds like it.

F: And if you were not upset or pained about consequences to your actions?

L: Yes, there's the gong. I'm a walking, talking self-destruct machine. Wind me up and watch me evade enlightenment and get AIDS (mildly chuckling now and turning more sober). You know that I don't want AIDS, and I know I don't want AIDS, but AIDS is what I have. But, guess what, I will deal with that. I can hardly believe I am saying this, but that's actually what I feel.

F: That's terrific, just terrific.

L: And guess what else I got, thanks to you.

F: What?

L: (broad smile). Nothing! A whole magnificent lot of nothing, and it feels like the best something I have ever known.

F: Great, so is there anything to forgive?

L: No, the word no longer seems to fit anything.

F: Right, it never does because there is never anything to forgive. Enjoy your nothingness!

Loretta returned to the ashram and resumed her place next to the guru. Now, as she would tell me in later contacts, she feels her "nothingness" and feels good about being who she is, where she is. She pursued any number of immune boosting regimes to assure her health and as of this writing, some four years after, she remains in good health, no, in excellent health with no signs of disease imminent in any way.

"THE WAGES OF PERFECTION IS DEATH" OR "DOES ANYONE 'NEED' TO BE HAPPY?"

This rephrasing of the statement from Scripture seems to me to capture the spirit of that dialogue and the struggle of Loretta with herself. A "Waiting for Godot" pursuit of "paths" that purport to lead to the elusive goal of "perfection." Then there is the subsequent disillusion when the pursuit peters out into frustration and a feeling of "there must be something wrong with me" because I don't seem to be able to "get it." This becomes an ongoing leitmotif for humans, especially among those who choose to be active "seekers" of the right formula for happiness.

Now I don't rephrase the scriptural utterance to in any way imply that there is anything "bad" going on here about either the pursuit of illusions or death or any combination thereof. That would be just repeating the same unhappiness, wouldn't it. No, there is nothing wrong with whatever people come to believe might be best for them to do. But this book is about happiness and to the degree that you, dear reader, might at least be disabused of the notion that there is a "right" formula, incantation, path someplace that frames the one true manner in which happiness is to be had, to that extent the book will have served some purpose for you.

I do not want, as I have said in earlier chapters, for you to see your happiness as Loretta was seeing it, that is, as a problem to be agonized over: "Oh why am I not happy now that I know I "should" or am "supposed" to be happy. What's wrong with me that I "resist" my happiness? Isn't that typical of me and the curse of being myself (the unbearable wrongness of being). Oh, why am I not someone else who would be a person who would be able to be happy!" No, happiness is not any imperative or "moral" value that "needs" to be fulfilled for me or you or the world to be okay. Happiness is simply the OPPORTUNITY to be happy, if that's what you come to know. If not, all is well, even with you though you may continue to feel and believe otherwise. Naturally, I would love to see you surrender any pockets of reservation about your happiness and affirm it unconditionally for yourself. Why not? It IS yours.

What I have offered you, to repeat, is not a formula, but an understanding that either will or will not stand the empirical test of your own experience of it. If it becomes true for you and you know your happiness on the basis of what you have learned from a reading and practice of what is in this volume, then you won't need convincing in the face of your experience; you will be living your happiness and words will not matter. If that is not your experience from a reading and practice of this work, then you will know that too and you will either give it more time and effort, perhaps seek out an experienced Option practitioner to aid you in your enterprise, or move on to what seems more profitable to you. So be it. In any case, be assured you have my best wishes for your happiness, however you may find it.

"Say 'Yes' to happiness! Always, only say, 'Yes!' to happiness. Say 'Yes,' to happiness at all times in all places, and bring the blessings of happiness forward that will well up within you. Happiness is always present to you. Just say,

'Yes.' A nod will do. Do not worry. None of these truths needs to be known or understood by anyone who does not know them, but they are the greatest joy for those who do."23

Postscript: "The Fifteen Minute 'Cure' for Unhappiness"

While finishing up work on this book, and after having done several seminars, I received a call from a woman, no longer young, who spoke with an Eastern European accent. She queried me as follows (we will call her Miriam for the sake of this dialogue):

M: Are you Mister Mosca, the man who makes people happy?

F: This is Frank Mosca, how can I help you?

M: I was told by my cousin that you helped him to be happy. (We established that her cousin had recently been in one of my workshops and had profited by it and shared her experience with Miriam). So, is it true you can make me happy?

F: Well, I don't understand myself to be making anyone happy, but I do what I can to help people let go of the beliefs that they hold that they have to be unhappy.

M: Well, I should tell you, that I am at the airport and my plane leaves in a half hour; I should also tell you that I have no money at present to pay you. So what do you think, you still want to help me to be happy?

F: (Pause). Well, look, I don't know what we can do in whatever time you have, but let's see what happens. First, tell me what specifically you are unhappy about?

M: What? *Mein Gott*, we don't have enough time to tell you.

F: Well, tell me what you can and we will take it from there.

M: To begin with, I am a survivor of the Holocaust. I lived, but all my family, mother, father, brother, sisters, they all perished. The Nazis killed everything, took everything and when it was over I was bereft of everything. From there it got no better. I married another survivor, a man who wasn't too happy to begin with, but who lived the remainder of his life with me in a misery that was hard as nails, like an apple that had been squeezed into a stone. Thank God, excuse me for saying, but he finally died. Now I feel like a stone myself, nothing gets in, nothing gets out. Just unhappy, unhappy, unhappy all the time (starts to cry).

F: Look, Miriam, I don't normally work quite this way, but tell me directly, do you want to be happy?

M: Happy, yes, if only God willing, that could be for me. That's why I called you.

F: Yes, good, I know. Then let me ask you this question. Despite all you have told me of your life, the destruction of your family, your marriage to someone who lived a stonelike life, despite all this you tell me you want to be happy. Then, what about all of this is something you feel you have to be unhappy about?

M: What about all of this? In what way could all of this be anything but what it was, what it is, all of it like a great weight that leaves no room to breathe much less to have happiness.

F: Well, okay, but listen, you did say you wanted to be happy didn't you? You wouldn't lie to yourself about that would you?

M: Lie, no, it is indeed happiness that I want.

F: Then let me ask you this question. Despite all that happened to you in your life, what might you be afraid would happen if you were not unhappy about all of that?

M: (fairly long pause). Not unhappy. God, it should only be. But how could I let go of all of that, wouldn't the memories, the people rise up in protest against my feeling good?

F: Are you saying that to surrender your lifelong misery would be an affront to all those who perished?

M: (Another pause). Such a way of thinking about this never entered my mind before. If only God could grant it be true.

F: You mention God a lot, Miriam, so let me ask you, do you think God wants your unhappiness over whatever happened, no matter what that was?

M: God, well, no. God never wants unhappiness. (pause) So, if God didn't want it, need it, then what? What about me then, no?

F: What do you think Miriam, would it mean anything about you were you to be happy right now, right in this minute, right where you stand?

M: (A long pause ensued, so much so that I finally asked if she were still on the line. Finally a voice full of emotion and wonder came back). I'M STUNNED.

F: I'm sorry, I don't think I heard you clearly, what did you say?

M: I said I'M STUNNED!

F: Yes, Miriam, but what does that mean? How do you feel right now?

M: (literally bursting through the wires in a mixture of what seemed to me like ecstasy still wrapped in the threads of disbelief at the possibility of having a feeling that just an instant ago seemed absolutely improbable). I'M HAPPY! I say it with such surprise, but that is what I feel. I'm amazed, how could that be?

F: Remember I asked you a moment ago would you lie to yourself about wanting happiness? Well, do you think you could lie to yourself about feeling this way?

M: No, no, it has been so long; there can be no doubt about what I feel, but tell me, will I be this way from now on?

F: What would stop you from being that way?

M: Nothing I guess, it's just so unfamiliar a feeling for me after all this time, so I don't want to lose it.

F: Then why would you?

M: I won't.

F: Each moment is the only moment there is, Miriam. And, in each moment you can live that feeling now that you know that it is always yours to live without restraint or regret.

M: So now my plane is leaving, so I must say goodbye. Be well and you have my gratitude for helping me with my happiness.

F: Be well and enjoy living your happiness, Miriam.

DO YOU WANT TO BE HAPPY?

This example is perhaps unusual in that by far not everyone is ready to give up their unhappiness so quickly. But what it serves to illustrate is that you never know. Given Miriam's life, many would have assumed that with such resume of pain and misery, she would be the most unlikely candidate for so swift a transformation. But, as I said earlier in this volume, life is all assumptions. We allow ourselves to be intimidated by what appears to be the case, usually based on our own presuppositions about what people are supposed to be able to do with their experiences. Miriam, despite all that one might say she brought to the conversation in terms of her past, was ready for her happiness. She did not know that herself until she was asked in the way Option has of asking about such things. Then she literally leapt upon the chance to let go of her "hard as nails" pain, as she called it. As we underestimate the ability of others to surmount what our beliefs might tell us is insurmountable, so too do we do the same with our own lives. You may at this very moment be ready for your happiness. Like a ripe, juicy apple, it may be hanging from the tree of your life. This is an opportunity to do just exactly the opposite of what, mythically, Adam and Eve did in the Garden of Eden. There, they sought to know what was wrong with life by eating the apple. When they did, they then thought they had discovered the inevitability of unhappiness; thus did they "lose" Paradise. Here is your chance to grasp the apple of your happiness. What you could know by biting deeply into the firm, ripe flesh of this fruit is your HAPPINESS. Like Miriam and so many others, you could know it now and through all the nows that you may be privileged to know, and that, for you, is FOREVER!

Appendix

Exploring Belief Paths

I have always wanted to write an "Appendix" to a book. Maybe it's because, as my client Marty might quip, I had mine removed when I was a child and never got over the "trauma." At any rate, the material contained herein is meant only to be adjunctive to your understanding of the Option Method. Remember, the heart of the procedure is in the simplicity of the Method itself. But, if for some of you, this review of the dialogues, the identification of beliefs, and the diagrams that are meant to summarize the "unhappy" universe vs. the "happy" one are of any help, then I invite you to make use of them.

To repeat, in this section we will explore what I have termed belief paths. This is just a way of aiding in the process of self-examination so that you can expose and hopefully surrender your beliefs about unhappiness. The beliefs will be highlighted in italics so that you can clearly see the list and progression of them and where they lead for that particular individual. The assertions and knowing of happiness will also be highlighted in the same way. This will also give you a ready reference to major belief patterns that more than likely will surface in aspects of your own existence. Not all beliefs obviously are going to be operative all the time; many are context-bound and arise therefore only in certain situations. But, the deeper one travels, usually the broader the belief base is, so that one reaches into assumptions that are more all encompassing and wide ranging as the assumptive architecture of our unhappiness reveals itself.

DIALOGUE ONE:

Note how with Sally the beginning belief was essentially that of Guilt, i.e., *of not doing or being a way that I am supposed to be*. Also note that the overall operating belief is out of our fear of becoming unhappy, *since I have been unhappy in the past, that must mean (I am afraid) I will be unhappy in the future*.

Then it progressed to her fear of being "unfair" to her partner, meaning, in a variation of the earlier belief, *I would not be being a way I was supposed to be toward another*. This of course leads directly to obligation, i.e., *I have to be a way that someone wants me to be, otherwise I am being a way I ought not to be, i.e., bad (for me and for others)*.

Now comes the Option experience that gradually sees Sally changing her beliefs and feelings, i.e., *I would not be wrong for me or for others if I were not to feel obliged. I don't need my pain of guilt to know what I know. I choose gratitude freely and am allowing of the other to be whatever way he/she feels comfortable being. He/she doesn't have to be any way for me nor I for him/her. That is true compassion.*

DIALOGUE TWO:

Allen begins with "I fucked up" meaning *I was bad for me by being exactly the way that I know to be*. This leads to regret which is repeated until there is the acknowledgement, through the taking of an Option, that *I was doing all I knew to do*.

Still, the issue of feeling pained remained and the Option came up to surrender the pain. Here, the belief *I must not feel happy because that would mean I did not care, i.e., am ultimately bad for me and for others*, is exposed. Notice how the beliefs throughout the dialogues circle and return to the central sense of the "rightness" or "wrongness" of the self. Notice how he moves from anger at her leaving to fear that, because she doesn't love him, *it must mean something about me*. This is pursued until he exercises his Option to surrender that belief; then what comes up is the issue of his liking/not liking. This is something he did not feel free to do. He expressed his fear of not liking on the grounds that it meant something about him *not to like*. He saw not liking as incompatible with loving. This leads him to compassion for his wife, since she also was being judged by him as being a way she *ought not to be*; so that despite his claim of having "fucked up" he harbored anger and resentment that his wife also was being a way she *ought not to be* and that this was depriving *him* of his ability to love, by virtue of her being that way. It was her responsibility to be a way *she was supposed to be so that he could love her*. This "codependence" of unhappy assumptions by couples merely reflects their individual fears about their own worthiness.

But, once not liking was okay, he could experience his FREEDOM to like and love or not as he wished. So we could know that there is nothing wrong with "fucking up," whatever the consequences, and at the same time we are perfectly free not to like our "fucking up" or the consequences or anything else for that matter without any of that compromising our happiness.

DIALOGUE THREE:

Terri's first belief is her shame which she describes as *feeling bad*. The suspicion is, without being directly seen initially, that *she* was the *cause* of unwanted attention. Notice how, again, the unhappy belief "law of gravity" brings us down to the *self*, experienced as somehow innately "bad" or flawed. Inside this circle of assumptions about the self is the illusory, but, once believed, extraordinarily powerful vortex of the *unbearable wrongness of being experience*, the most basic dread of somehow discovering that all the worst assumptions about the self are true.

When questioned about her unhappiness further, she replies defensively that she did not want what she did not want, as if there was any reason to feel that this was not a legitimate way to be. Now, she expresses her sense of helplessness at *being wrong for being who she was*. In so believing she found her only hope to be that the other would not have been who he was. This is the sense of being *stuck*. Then the Option is presented to feel okay. This allows her to see that her unhappiness is what she holds onto because she believed it would have been only a confirmation of her *being bad for herself were she to contradict the unhappiness that others believed she should feel over what happened.* She now sees past that and surrenders that unhappiness to become open to welcoming her happy state. In so doing, she *shatters her status as a prisoner of a victim mentality, which is so highly invested in as a prized way to be in our time, that compromising our happiness.*

DIALOGUE FOUR:

Stephanie begins with the unhappiness of self doubt, a feeling/belief which immediately brings up the question *can I be bad for me?* She says that she is faced with this doubt because the universe is a way it should not be, i.e., it is a universe that allows bodies to become what we call sick, in this case cancerous. This is the root of the belief called *unfairness, i.e., things, again, are a way they should not be.*

From this, she moves to the fear of being foolish in *being a way that others would disapprove of* which leads back to the fear that I could be bad for me, i.e., my "stupidity" in making the choices I make could result in my death! The Option opportunity comes in acknowledging that her undertaking is the result of the best intelligence she knows to apply to her self preservation, that is, she is making the best choice she can based on the information she currently has.

Now the issue runs to another variant of why it is not appropriate to be happy: *I must be crazy to be happy in the face of all others who believe that to be unhappy is the appropriate way to be.* An Option opportunity comes to surrender the belief that it is in any way ever wrong to be happy. She does this, but what remains is a fantasy that even after death she would somehow still be subject to the judgement of others. She takes the opportunity to surrender that belief by recognizing it as just another variant of believing that *I could be a way I don't want to be against my will.* Now, without reservation, she accepts her happiness.

DIALOGUE FIVE:

Ronnie begins with general bad feelings and then specifies his *fear of being a loser.* Proof of this is the behavior and choices of others who are following a more conventional path.

The Option offer is to ask whether he feels obliged to feel bad because others disapprove. He clarifies that he doesn't want to feel bad. But *how could I feel good when others disapprove. I am afraid it would mean something about me,* i.e., reflecting a core concern of being "bad" or flawed. The Option clarification comes in his embracing that he doesn't want to feel that way and testing it empirically *by actually feeling okay inside.*

What is left is an issue with his father; he cannot seem to be a way that his father would approve of, and, in turn, his father *is being a way he ought not to be in disapproving of Ronnie, so as to make it thereby impossible to love him.* The father's not loving exposes Ronnie's belief that *there must be something wrong with me, lacking in me , such that it makes me impossible to be loved!* The Option which emerges for Ronnie is that this is not true, and that part of the role of feeling bad about his father is to *stay in touch with his caring about him.* So, again, *to feel unhappy means to be caring* gets exposed as an important belief.

Finally, the question of *not doing what I want* emerges and the Option clarification appears for Ronnie when he knows that his unhappiness is meant to motivate him to do what he says he wants to do. So, *without the pain and distress, I would not do for myself what I thought best to do!* This in turn rests on *therefore I could be bad for me without the unhappiness to hold me in check.* Once having let that go, he takes possession of his good feelings.

DIALOGUE SIX:

Marty starts out believing *there must be something wrong with me.* The proof is in what he describes as "symptoms" and the confirmation of others who all have different reasons for affirming this. As this is explored in various guises, he gets to expose fear and pain over his failed marriage, where he takes lack of interest as proof there is something wrong with him. Obviously, as it seems to him, *he is being a way he is not supposed to be.* From this comes a fear of wanting because if I could be bad for me, then it would be *dangerous to want.* Also not getting what he wants is proof of this. Yet he sees, through an Option awareness, that *it would be okay not to be unhappy about this and that feelings follow immediately when beliefs shift.*

Doubts remain about the legitimacy of feeling happy in the face of still unfulfilled wants. Now the notion of being *crazy not to be unhappy about not getting what you want* arises. The momentum of his already aroused Option awareness allows him to surrender this, and again immediately there is a shift to good feelings. Then the question of the "future" as a possible *time when he would not feel a way he would want to feel arises.* It is addressed from the perspective of seeing the future as a mere hypothesis, while the *present is the only time anyone lives in.* Marty's acceptance of this for himself releases any final reservations about his ability *to be happy or to remember to be happy at any given moment of his existence.*

DIALOGUE SEVEN:

Monique opens with the fear of potential exposure of some past behavior that would result in her having to *feel unhappy against her will.* She complains that the world is unfair, i.e., *a way it ought not to be* and because *I was a way I shouldn't have been,* now, at least potentially I would make myself unlovable to my husband. Her Option insights from previous work get her quickly beyond that, since she had already dealt with her father about the same belief pattern. Several beliefs fall by the wayside, including requiring that *another be a way I want him to be for my happiness*, which is a version of *if you loved me you would be the way I want you to be , so I could love you!*

The issue of her husband's father and his character is then dealt with. This shifts quickly to fears of pain and death as a "terrible thing." At the same time Monique is feeling that *she must feel bad about that and at the same time feels guilty that she doesn't like the man.* She easily grasps that and surrenders it . She ends with a fear for her and her children's' future. Her belief in God is explored and she comes to see through her own understanding of death and God, that *all would be well and her happiness is hers no matter what the circumstances because that truly is the nature of reality.*

DIALOGUE EIGHT:

Loretta's plaint is that "bliss" eludes her and that life has no meaning. The proof of this is essentially that she has not gotten what she wanted. This shifts into *therefore there must be something wrong with me otherwise I would have "gotten it" by now.* The Option questioning helps to get to the next belief that *she must maintain her despair as a means of knowing she wants better out of life.* This "edge" as she calls it, now unfolds itself as a life long belief that *only through her not getting what she wants can she have permission to curse the universe for being a way it ought not to be.*

She is so upset with this that she comes to the point of leaving, but agrees to take the Option to explore her inner feelings to see what it might be like to feel otherwise. What follows is a breakthrough in her experience as she feels "nothing." This "nothing" she comes to know as simply her experience of good feelings, the feelings that had been "eluding" her for decades. This great release is tempered by some remaining beliefs that she was a phoney in presenting herself to be a way that she actually was not truly feeling inside. The Option understanding of *doing the best she knew* always gets her beyond this belief to the prospect of dying from AIDS, the last stumbling block to feeling okay.

Exploration of this leads to a *fear of the disapproval of others*, the first element in a belief trail which includes the ongoing motif that my choices in life prove that I must be bad for me. At first she responds to the Option questions as if not to care i.e., not be unhappy about that, would isolate her and *how would I know I wanted the company of others if I were not pained at the prospect of not having it?* This gets her past the disapproval of others to the disapproval of herself. Having AIDS is the ultimate proof of *her being bad for herself*, hence "bad" at the core. Returning to her Option understanding of *doing the best she can always*, she moves past this to embrace her happiness in a realm where forgiveness is precisely to know that *there is not nor ever could be anything to forgive because all is the way it is supposed to be (given all the beliefs, choices, behaviors and motions of the physical universe prior to this moment) always was the way it was supposed to be and could never be anything other than the way it will (is supposed to) be!* THIS IS THE OPTION "GUARANTEE." YOU WILL ALWAYS BE DOING EXACTLY WHAT YOU WANT IN A WORLD THAT IS EXACTLY THE WAY IT IS SUPPOSED TO BE AND EVEN IF YOU DO NOT TO LIKE ANY OF IT, YOUR HAPPINESS IS ASSURED!

POSTSCRIPT:

In this dialogue one major belief stood out above any other. Miriam believed *that to be happy would be a deep betrayal of all those who perished; that her unhappiness was the ongoing badge of her dedication to the dead and her affirmation that she profoundly did not like any of what had occurred.* She expected nothing but unhappiness as in the way she described her husband's lifelong stance. However, there was in her always a deep desire to be happy. What she lacked was some way to give herself permission to experience her happiness, especially against the enormous historical backdrop of the Holocaust. Her faith in God as a God who is Happiness was the key that unlocked the "dungeon" of her belief that she had to maintain solidarity with the suffering of millions by suffering herself. But in the face of a God who is Happiness she realized she could trust her knowing that she did not like what she did not like and still open her heart up to the infinite wellsprings of her own happiness and joy. Truly a miracle of compassion of one person for themselves.

NOTE: By no means is the analysis of these dialogues exhaustive. You may find nuances of other belief patterns at work. Enjoy your search and your exploration of your own beliefs as well.

Primal Dread and Primal Awe: A Tale of Two Worldviews.

PRIMAL DREAD: "The Invisible Spheres Were Formed in Fright!"
Melville' s Moby Dick

A "DANTEAN" VISION OF AN UNHAPPY UNIVERSE: AN INVERTED
PYRAMID OF ASSUMPTIONS ALWAYS FUNNELING DOWN TO SOME PRIMAL
STATE THAT MUST BE AVOIDED AT ALL COSTS, AS IF TO KNOW IT WOULD
BE TO KNOW THE "TERRIBLE TRUTH" ABOUT THE NATURE OF THE
UNIVERSE, I.E., THAT IT IS FUNDAMENTALLY UNHAPPY.
SURFACE SYMPTOMS OF UNHAPPINESS: Fears, phobias, frustra-
tions, rages, grief, related physical symptoms; feelings of compulsion,
obsession, paranoia, helplessness, depression, anxiety etc., etc.

Are created by beliefs which are experienced, when described in terms
of language, as *needs, shoulds, musts, oughts, have to's, obligations, demands,*
etc. which apply to us, to other people, all socio-political entities, and all
aspects of the physical universe as well,

Which, if not carried out, observed, fulfilled (and remember, this often
does not depend on us, but on the motions of the physical world, the

inclinations of others to give us what we want, or to affirm us in some way or to deny us and reject us if they so wish) by us or by others, or the physical universe,

Become the occasion for our choosing to believe any number of things about ourselves, others and the very nature of being, existence itself, the most common of which are: *there must be something wrong with me, otherwise people would respond to me in a way that I would want them to; or, I am not being a way I am supposed to be and that is why I make it impossible for others to love me;* interpersonally: *if others really loved me they would be a way I want them to be so that I would be able to love them; or, if I am not unhappy, in whatever form that might take, I would lose the motivation to do things that I say I want, know I want, but would not actually somehow really want without the pain of my distress to prod me to go after what I want; or, since I do not always get what I want, I must be unhappy about that, else I will not be moved to continue to go after what I want. In such instances, my wants are more aptly described as "needs," since the word implies that it is a requirement in order for me to be happy, since how could I be happy without something that I "need"?*

Additionally, *not getting what I need/want must be proof of my basic unworthiness haplessness, fatal flaw; it may also mean that I cannot trust me to know what I want, since it is clear that I could want things that others might consider "bad" or "wrong"; therefore, I could be "bad" for me and it could be dangerous for me to want. An extension of this is that I am not free to like or dislike things, since my judgment is fundamentally flawed by my inclination to make choices that are bad for me. This leads deeper into the core sense of ontological wrongness, i.e., not only am I fundamentally a way I am not supposed to be, but I exist in a universe which is also fundamentally a way it is not supposed to be. I not only can experience feelings I do not want to feel against my will, but I can cause others to experience feelings they do not want against their will. The name we give to feelings that accompany these and other beliefs are , shame, guilt, regret, anguish, embarrassment, humiliation, victimization, hatred, loneliness, longing, squeamishness, outrage, terror, and so many more.*

As this spirals down into tighter and tighter coils of distress and dis-ease our sense of anticipatory dread grows apace. This brings us to the core of our beliefs about the inner horror of ourselves and the unhappy universe which is the stage on which that inner horror gets acted out in our lives, the state I call *PRIMAL DREAD.* Here is the very center of the circle of unhappiness which is the realm of *EVIL,* or the sense that we can be made to feel feelings we do not wish to feel against our will and can do the same to others. That we are fundamentally somehow *AGAINST OURSELVES* at the very root! Here is the heart of *DESPAIR:*

THE UNBEARABLE WRONGNESS OF BEING!

PRIMAL AWE:

BY CONTRAST, IN A HAPPY UNIVERSE, THE ASSUMPTIONS SPIRAL OUTWARD FROM SEVERAL CORE UNDERSTANDINGS ABOUT THE NATURE OF WHAT IS:

AT THE CORE: THE TRUTH OF BEING: *HAPPINESS IS, EVEN AS BEING SIMPLY IS!*

FROM THIS IS GENERATED *PRIMAL AWE!*

From this sense of deepest resonance and congruence with that truth we come to know that concepts such as *FREEDOM, LOVE, TRUTH, COMPASSION* and related notions are simply different aspects of that central truth of being. Knowing this can generate any number of experiences of *ECSTASY, JOY, ELATION.*

Additionally, we are thereby imbued by our knowingness of the truth of Happiness with an ongoing and evolving *ATTITUDE* which becomes the living instrument of whatever we create for ourselves, or what we create in concert with others. In carrying out the basic knowingness of the Attitude, we know that it could never be somehow "wrong" to be happy at any time. We know that we do not have to accept anything about others or the world, that we can like and not like with equal abandon and know it never imperils our equanimity. We can live a life filled with gratitude but free of any compulsion or sense of obligation. We can love whom we wish, as we wish, and never be concerned about reciprocity or conditions. It is the creature of our unbridled spontaneity, never to be caged by the chains of another's, or a culture's requirements to love. Our love of the world, all in it, the universe, if we so choose, is our gift to ourselves!

Thus in all we do, we can bring a sense of playfulness which is simply the moment to moment knowing that all is the way that it is and that it need not be any other way for our happiness, even though we may not like anything that is going on in any particular moment. Our intensities of playfulness, or joy, or affection spring from our Attitude of knowing our happiness. We have chosen to surrender our beliefs about unhappiness and thus are free to take full possession, in our own idiosyncratic, utterly personal and irreproducible way of the fullness of whatever our happiness might come to mean to us at any given instant. Each instant is all that there is and contains within it the fullness of truth, wisdom, beauty , love and happiness beyond measure, so that we can never exhaust the wholeness of any moment. IT IS ETERNITY NOW! IT IS OUR HAPPINESS FOREVER NOW!

Notes

These notes make reference to material that Bruce Di Marsico made available to advanced students of the Option Method. None is presently available. Some of this material may be included in the publication of his works as the opportunity presents itself in the future.

1   *Understanding the Option Method*, "Unhappiness is not Wrong." p. 2.
2   *A Brief Compendium of the Option Method*. pg. 11.
3   *A Brief Compendium...* pg. 2
4   *A Brief Compendium...* pg. 9
5   *The Basis*. pg. 7
6   *Teachings: A Series of Instructions on the Option Method.*
7   *The Basis*. pg. 4.
8   *Understanding the Option Method.* "On Owing and Debts, and Freedom, Forgiveness, and Gifts."
9   *All You Need To Know About Your Life.* "Proof we are 'Bad'," pg. 2.
10 *The Basis*. pg. 13.
11 *Speculations: A Series of Meditations on Happiness.* "The Enjoyment of Happiness."
12 *Teachings: A Series of Instructions on the Option Method.* "Allowed to Be." pg. 3.
13 *All You Need To Know About Your Life.*, pg. 3.
14 *The Creation of the Option Method and the Nature of Happiness.* pg. 8
15 *A Brief Compendium....* pg. 19.
16 *The Basis*, pg. 7.

17 *A Brief Compendium*.... pg. 21.

18 *A Brief Compendium*.... pg. 17.

19 *The Basis*. pg. 14.

20 *A Brief Compendium*.... pg. 14.

21 *Option Theology*. pp. 1,2.

22 *The Creation of the Option Method and The Nature of Happiness*. pg. 9.

23 *Option Theology*. pg. 3.

About the Author

Frank Mosca Ph.D. is an Option Educator with a private practice in Hampton Bays, N.Y. He has a background in the Humanities as a former Professor at N.Y. University, and in Psychology, having received Graduate and Post Graduate training at N.Y. University Post Doctoral Institute for Psychotherapy and other institutions. He has published on topics as varied as hypnosis, altered states and chaos theory. After years of training with Bruce Di Marsico the founder of the Option Method, Frank now lectures locally and nationally. Additional works include *The Joybuilding Workbook*, *The Unbearable Wrongness of Being*, and a novel, *The God Speak*.

Printed in the United States
63939LVS00004B/349

9 780595 157808